Max ....

The **Arsonists**

in a new translation by

Alistair Beaton

Methuen Drama

Methuen Drama Modern Plays

1 3 5 7 9 8 6 4 2

This translation first published in 2007 by Methuen Drama

Methuen Drama
A & C Black Publishers Limited
38 Soho Square
London W1D 3HB

Original work entitled *Biedermann und die Brandstifter*
copyright © 1958 by Suhrkamp Verlag, Frankfurt am Main
Translation copyright © 2007 by Alistair Beaton

Alistair Beaton has asserted his moral right to be identified
as the author of this work

A CIP catalogue record for this book is available
from the British Library

ISBN 978 1 408 10393 7

Typeset by Country Setting, Kingsdown, Kent
Printed and bound in Great Britain by
Cox & Wyman Ltd, Reading, Berkshire

ROYAL COURT

Royal Court Theatre presents

THE ARSONISTS

by **Max Frisch**
in a new translation by **Alistair Beaton**

First performance at Royal Court Jerwood Theatre Downstairs, Sloane Square,
London on 1 November 2007.

Media Partner

THE
INDEPENDENT

THE ARSONISTS

by **Max Frisch**

in a new translation by **Alistair Beaton**

Anna **Zawe Ashton**
Chorus **Michael Begley**
Schmitz **Paul Chahidi**
Eisenring **Benedict Cumberbatch**
Babette **Jacqueline Defferary**
Chorus **David Hinton**
Biedermann **Will Keen**
Chorus/Doctor of Philosophy **Munir Khairdin**
Chorus **Claire Prempeh**
Chorus/Widow Knechtling **Alwyne Taylor**
Chorus Leader **Graham Turner**

Director **Ramin Gray**
Designer **Anthony Ward**
Lighting Designer **Johanna Town**
Sound Designer **Christopher Shutt**
Choreography **Hofesh Shechter**
Assistant Director **Katharina Wienecke**
Casting Director **Amy Ball**
Production Manager **Paul Handley**
Stage Manager **Tariq Sayyid Rifaat**
Deputy Stage Manager **Sarah Tryfan**
Assistant Stage Manager **Sarah Lyndon**
Stage Management Work Placement **Ruth Murfitt**
Costume Supervisor **Iona Kenrick**
Set Built by **Miraculous Engineering**

The Royal Court and Stage Management wish to thank the following for their help with this production: Brigitte Auer, Lucy at Bottlegreen, Coleman's Mustard, all the staff at Euston Firestation, The International Cheese Centre, Rebecca Krajniewski, Grape Juice kindly donated by Welch's www.welchsjuice.co.uk.

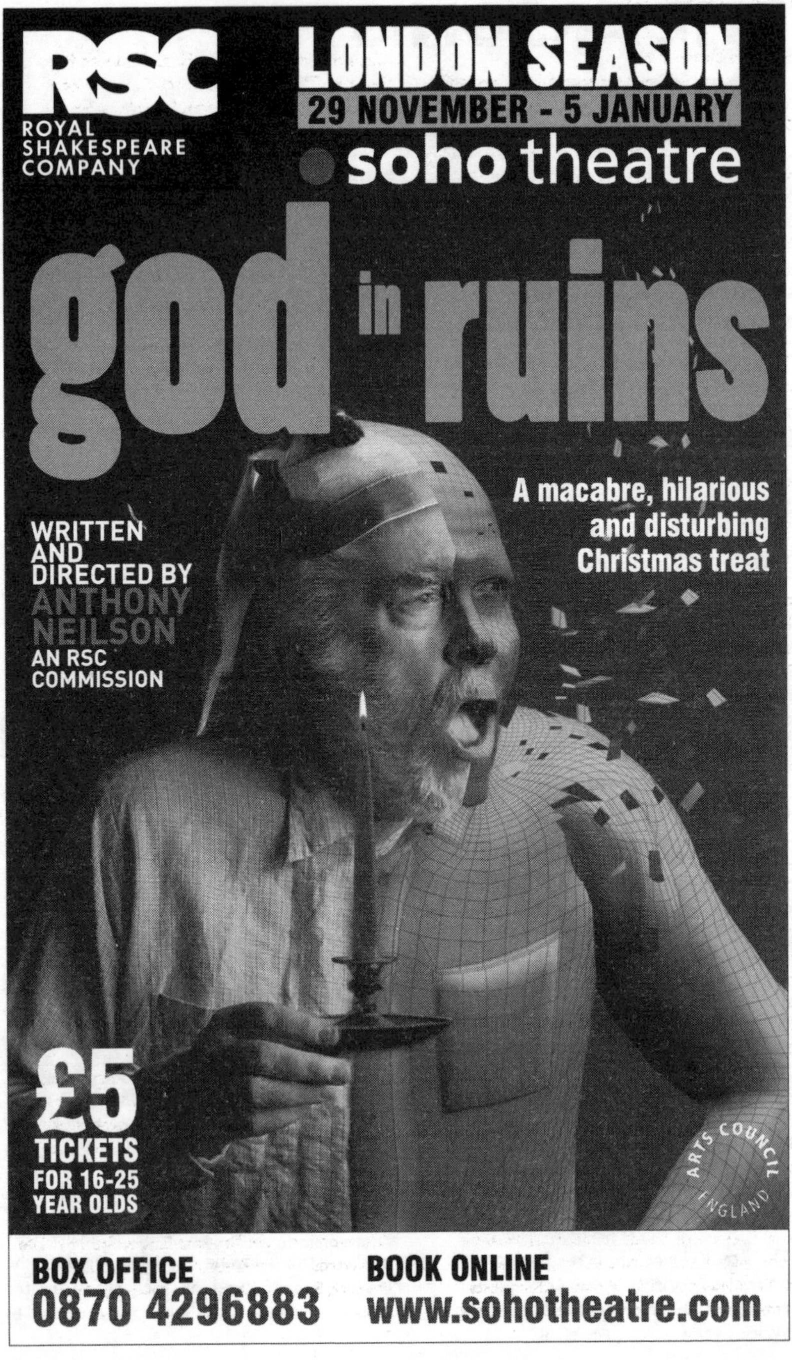
RSC
ROYAL
SHAKESPEARE
COMPANY
LONDON SEASON
29 NOVEMBER - 5 JANUARY
soho theatre
god in ruins
A macabre, hilarious
and disturbing
Christmas treat
WRITTEN
AND
DIRECTED BY
ANTHONY
NEILSON
AN RSC
COMMISSION
£5
TICKETS
FOR 16-25
YEAR OLDS
ARTS COUNCIL
ENGLAND
BOX OFFICE
0870 4296883
BOOK ONLINE
www.sohotheatre.com

THE COMPANY

Max Frisch (writer)
The Arsonists was first performed in German under the title Biedermann und die Brandstifter in 1958. It premiered in English at the Royal Court on 21 December 1961 in a translation by Michael Bullock entitled The Fire Raisers. Other works include: Andorra, Biografie, Don Juan oder Die Liebe zur Geometrie, Die Chinesische Mauer, Nun Singen Sie Wieder, Santa Cruz, Als der Krieg zu Ende War, Graf Öderland, Jonas und Sein Veteran.

Alistair Beaton (translator)
Theatre includes: King of Hearts (Out of Joint/ Sonia Friedman Productions with Hampstead); Follow My Leader (Birmingham Rep/ Hampstead); Feelgood (Hampstead/Garrick). Translations and adaptations include: The Government Inspector (Chichester Festival); Die Fledermaus, La Vie Parisienne (D'Oyly Carte); The Nose (Nottingham Playhouse). Television includes: The Trial of Tony Blair, A Very Social Secretary, Downwardly Mobile, Spitting Image, Minder, Not the Nine O'clock News. Radio includes: Fourth Column, The Beaton Generation, Dome Alone with Alistair Beaton, Little England Big World, as well as appearances on the Today Programme, PM, The World Tonight, Any Questions, The News Quiz and Front Row. Alistair Beaton is fluent in French, German and Russian.

Zawe Ashton
For the Royal Court: Rhinoceros, Gone Too Far! Theatre includes: Othello (Globe); The Cage (Nuffield, Southampton); Blue Moon Over Poplar, The Big Nickel (Soho); A Midsummer Night's Dream, Old Vic Gala (NYT). Television includes: Mobile, The Crust, Holby City, East Enders, NCS Manhunt, In Deep, The Bill, Wild House, Demon Headmaster, Game On. Film includes: Spiralling, Shooters.

Michael Begley
For the Royal Court: Rhinoceros. Other theatre includes: Who's Afraid of Virginia Woolf, Adam Geist, Mad for It (Manchester Royal Exchange); Pravda (Chichester Festival/ Birmingham Rep.); Martha Loves Michael (Ruffian/Pleasance); The Norman Conquests (Birmingham Rep.); Hobson's Choice (Touring

Consortium/Birmingham Rep./Plymouth Royal); Flip Fest, The Tempest (Contact); Death of a Salesman, Wildest Dreams, Life of Galileo (Manchester Library); Deep Blue Sea (Nottingham Playhouse); One Day in October (Riverside Studios); Hunting Scenes from Lower Bavaria (Gate). Television includes: Miss Marple, Doctors, The Eleventh Hour, Wire in the Blood, The Bill, Dalziel and Pascoe, William and Mary, The Royal, Stretford Wives, Bob and Rose, In Deep, City Central, Heartbeat, The Grand II, Grafters, McLibel!, See You Friday, This Life, Hillsborough, London's Burning, Julius Caesar. Film includes: Vacuuming Completely Nude in Paradise.

Paul Chahidi
For the Royal Court: Rhinoceros. Other theatre includes: Faustus (Theatre Royal, Northampton); Merry Wives the Musical, As You Like It, The American Pilot, A Midsummer Night's Dream, Cymbeline, The Taming of the Shrew, The Tamer Tamed, The Devil is an Ass, Julius Caesar, Faust, Woyzeck (RSC); Engaged (Orange Tree); Twelfth Night, Macbeth, The Two Noble Kinsmen, The Comedy of Errors, Augustine's Oak (Globe); Arabian Nights (Young Vic); Misalliance (Clwyd); All's Well That Ends Well (Oxford Stage Co.); George Dandin, Jungle Book (Redgrave, Farnham); Stiff (Pleasance); Next D.G. of the BBC (Simon Block). Television includes: Oliver Twist, Mary Whitehouse, Fear of Fanny, Blackpool, Murder in Mind, Murder Most Horrid, Blonde Bombshell, Bliss, Peak Practice, Wise Children. Film includes: Venus, The Libertine, Notting Hill, Stella Does Tricks. Radio includes: Felix Holt, On the Field, The Charterhouse of Parma, The Mel and Sue Thing.

Benedict Cumberbatch
For the Royal Court: Rhinoceros. Other theatre includes: Period of Adjustment, Lady from the Sea (Almeida); Hedda Gabler (Almeida/West End); Oh What a Lovely War, Romeo & Juliet, As You Like It, A Midsummer Night's Dream, Love's Labour's Lost (The New Shakespeare Co.); The Visit (Drayton Court, Ealing). Television includes: The Last Enemy, Stuart: A Life Backwards, To the Ends of the Earth, Hawking, Dunkirk, Spooks, Cambridge Spies, Tipping the Velvet.

Film includes: The Other Boleyn Girl, Atonement, Amazing Grace, Starter for Ten. Awards include: Best Actor Monte Carlo Television Festival 2004 for Hawking; Best Actor Monte Carlo Television Festival 2006 Golden Nymph Award for To the Ends of the Earth; Third Prize Ian Charleson Award for Hedda Gabler.

Jacqueline Defferary

For the Royal Court: Rhinoceros, Push Up, Our Late Night, Blue Heart (with Out of Joint/national tour), The Treatment.

Other theatre includes: Much Ado About Nothing, Under the Black Flag (Globe); Fen & Far Away (Sheffield); Homebody/Kabul, Lucifer and the Lord (Young Vic); The Rivals, Comedy of Errors (RSC); Cleo Camping Emmanuelle & Dick, The Skryker (National); The Importance of Being Earnest (Birmingham/Old Vic); Bed Before Yesterday (Almeida); What the Butler Saw (Salisbury).

Television includes: Kissing the Gunner's Daughter, Harry Enfield and Chums, Cor Blimey, A Life in Recipes – The Elizabeth David Story, Our Hidden Lives, The Bill.

Ramin Gray (director)

For the Royal Court: The Ugly One, Scenes from the Back of Beyond, Woman and Scarecrow, Motortown (& Wiener Festwochen), Way to Heaven, Bear Hug, The Weather, Ladybird, Advice to Iraqi Women, Terrorism, Night Owls, Just a Bloke, Push Up, How I Ate a Dog.

Other theatre includes: Am Strand der Weiten Welt (Volkstheater, Wien); King of Hearts (Hampstead with Out of Joint); The American Pilot (RSC); The Child, The Invisible Woman (Gate); Cat and Mouse (Sheep) (Théâtre National de l'Odéon, Paris/Gate); A Message for the Broken-Hearted (Liverpool Playhouse/BAC); At Fifty She Discovered the Sea, Harry's Bag, Pig's Ear, A View from the Bridge (Liverpool Playhouse).

Ramin is an Associate Director at the Royal Court.

David Hinton

For the Royal Court: Rhinoceros.

Other theatre includes: Antony & Cleopatra, In Extremis (Globe); Thomas Moore, A New Way to Please You, Believe What You Will, A Russian in the Woods, Twelfth Night, Jubilee, The Memory of Water (RSC); Home (Oxford Stage Co.); In Arabia We'd All Be Kings (Hampstead); The Herbal Bed (RSC/National tour); Veronica's Room (Palace, Westcliff); This Happy Breed (Marlowe, Canterbury); Veronica's Room (Ashcroft, Croydon); The Art of Success (Man in the Moon); The Railway Children (Duke's, Lancaster); The Wind in the Willows (tour); A Man for all Seasons (Liverpool Playhouse); Romeo and Juliet (tour); Electra (Shaw); Hamlet, The Winter's Tale (Compass); Waiting for Godot, Merchant of Venice (Compass/Far East); The Alchemist (Tokyo Globe); Dr Faustus (Oratory).

Television and film includes: National Treasure, Secret Life, Revolution, Bombshell, Casualty, The Upside of Anger, Doctors, The Bill, Out of Sight, The Knock, London's Burning, The Burden, Flap, The Challenge, Back Home Again.

Will Keen

Theatre includes: Kiss of the Spider Woman (Donmar); Tom & Viv, Five Gold Rings (Almeida); The Changeling (Barbican/tour); The Rubenstein Kiss (Hampstead); Don Juan, Man and Superman (Theatre Royal, Bath); Pericles (Lyric Hammersmith); Dido Queen of Carthage, The Tempest, Two Noble Kinsmen (Globe); The Duchess of Malfi, The Coast of Utopia, Hove, Mary Stuart (National); Prince of Homburg (Lyric, Hammersmith); A Midsummer Night's Dream (West End); The Seagull, Present Laughter, The Tempest (West Yorkshire Playhouse); Elton John's Glasses (West End/tour); Phaedra, Traveller Without Luggage, Little Creatures, Antigone, Resolution (BAC); Happy Valley (Liverpool Everyman); Shakuntala, The Boat Plays, Frank Juno (Gate); Merchant of Venice (Salisbury Playhouse); Gasping (Chester Gateway); A Midsummer Night's Dream, Forty Years On (Exeter Northcott); Much Ado About Nothing (Southwark Playhouse).

Television includes: Casualty 1907, The Colour of Magic, Elizabeth 1st, The Impressionists, Holby City, Murphy's Law, Into the Void, Monsignor Renard, The Bill, For Valour, Do The Right Thing, Martin Chuzzlewit, Between The Lines, Inspector Alleyn.

Film includes: Love and Other Disasters, The Nine Lives of Thomas Katz.

Munir Khairdin

For the Royal Court: Gone Too Far!

Other theatre includes: Foxes (West Yorkshire Playhouse); The Hot Zone, (Lyric Hammersmith); Calcutta Kosher (Kali Theatre Co.); Behzti (Birmingham Rep.); Bombay Dreams (Apollo Victoria); Romeo & Juliet (Hazlitt Open Air); Rashoman, Butcher's Skin (Yellow Earth); The Trial, Merchant of Venice (Cherub Co.); Romeo & Juliet (Leicester Haymarket).

Film and television includes: The Passion, Britz, Rendition, It Was an Accident, Spooks.

Claire Prempeh
For the Royal Court: Rhinoceros.
Other theatre includes: generations (Young Vic);
Orestes (Shared Experience); Catseyes.com
(Derngate, Northampton).

Hofesh Schechter (choreographer)
For the Royal Court: Motortown.
Other theatre includes: Saint Joan (National);
In Your Rooms (The Place/Southbank Centre/
Sadler's Wells); Uprising, Bare Bones Company
season, Edge season, Cult (The Place); Fragments
(Resolution! 2004 Festival/tour).
Television includes: Skins.
Hofesh was Associate Artist at The Place
2004-2006 and is currently Artist in Residence
at The Point in Eastleigh.

Christopher Shutt (sound designer)
Theatre includes: Warhorse, Philistines,
Chatroom/Citizenship, Happy Days, A Dream
Play, Measure for Measure, Mourning Becomes
Electra, Humble Boy, Play Without Words,
Albert Speer, Not About Nightingales, Machinal
(National); Coram Boy (National/Broadway);
The Elephant Vanishes, A Minute Too Late,
Mnemonic, Street of Crocodiles, Three Lives of
Lucie Cabrol, Caucasian Chalk Circle
(Complicite); A Disappearing Number
(Complicite with Barbican); Strange Poetry
(Complicite with LA Philharmonic); Noise of
Time (Complicite with Emerson Quartet);
All About My Mother (Old Vic); The Bacchae
(National Theatre of Scotland); Moon for the
Misbegotten (Old Vic/Broadway); Julius Caesar
(Barbican); Hecuba, Phaedra (Donmar);
The Resistible Rise of Arturo Ui (New York).
Radio includes: A Shropshire Lad, After the
Quake.
Awards include: Two New York Drama Desk
Awards for Outstanding Sound Design for Not
About Nightingales and Mnemonic.
Christopher has been Head of Sound at the
Bristol Old Vic, the Royal Court and the
National. He is now freelance and is a regular
collaborator with Theatre de Complicite.

Alwyne Taylor
For the Royal Court: Rhinoceros.
Other theatre includes: Guys and Dolls
(Donmar/Ambassadors/tour); Diamond
(King's Head); Stallerhof (Southwark Playhouse);
Platonov, The Bed Before Yesterday (Almeida);
David Copperfield, A Small Family Business
(West Yorkshire Playhouse); The Nun, Spring
Awakening (BAC), Richard III (Pleasance);
A Chorus of Disapproval, Revenger's Comedies,
The Linden Tree, June Moon, Last of the Red

Hot Lovers (Stephen Joseph, Scarborough);
Trial by Jury (Covent Garden Festival); Swollen
Tongues (Cochrane); A Christmas Carol
(Liverpool Playhouse); Blithe Spirit (Exeter);
Three Sisters (Bristol Old Vic); The Constant
Wife (Windsor); Two, Tess of the D'Urbevilles,
See How They Run (Derby Playhouse);
The Norman Conquests (Crucible); Abigail's
Party, Top Girls (Bolton); Gateway to Heaven
(The Oval); Pat and Margaret (New Vic, Stoke);
Day in the Death of Joe Egg (Sherman, Cardiff);
The Rover (Salisbury); Once in a Life Time,
Company, Sweet Charity, Accrington Pals
(Library, Manchester); Home, Stepping Out
(Oldham).
Television includes: Midsomer Murders,
Emmerdale, East Enders, Heartbeat, Casualty,
The Bill, Devices and Desires, Strong Poison,
Is That a Fact?.
Film includes: The Old Curiosity Shop, Asylum.
Radio includes: The Healing Art, The Outside
Child, Diary of a Provincial Lady, The Golden
Triangle.

Johanna Town (lighting designer)
For the Royal Court: Over 50 productions,
including Rhinoceros, My Child, Scenes from the
Back of Beyond, My Name is Rachel Corrie
(& West End/Galway Festival/Edinburgh Festival/
Minetta Lane, New York), Rainbow Kiss,
The Winterling, The Woman Before, Way To
Heaven, A Girl in a Car With a Man, Under the
Whaleback, The Kitchen, O Go My Man (with
Out of Joint), Talking to Terrorists (with Out of
Joint), Shopping and Fucking (with Out of Joint/
West End), The Steward of Christendom (with
Out of Joint/Broadway).
Other theatre includes: Guantanamo (Tricycle/
West End/New York); Rose (National/New
York); Arabian Nights, Our Lady of Sligo (New
York); Little Malcolm and His Struggle Against
the Eunuchs (West End/Hampstead); Feelgood,
Top Girls, Via Dolorosa, Beautiful Thing (West
End); Triumph of Love, All the Ordinary Angels
(Royal Exchange); To Kill A Mocking Bird
(Birmingham Rep/tour); The Glassroom
(Hampstead); King of Hearts (Out of Joint/
Hampstead); The Overwhelming, The Permanent
Way, She Stoops to Conquer (Out of Joint/
National); Macbeth (Out of Joint world tour);
In Praise of Love (Chichester); Dead Funny
(West Yorkshire Playhouse); How Love is Spelt
(Bush); I.D. (Almeida/BBC3); Badnuff (Soho);
The Dumb Waiter (Oxford).
Recent opera includes: Cinderella (Scottish
Opera); The Marriage of Figaro (Classical Opera
Company).
Jo is Head of Lighting at the Royal Court.

Graham Turner

For the Royal Court: Rhinoceros.
Other theatre includes: Comfort Me With
Apples (Hampstead); Enemies (Almeida); 5/11,
Government Inspector, Scapino, A Midsummer
Night's Dream, Master and Marguerita
(Chichester Festival); Girl in the Goldfish Bowl
(Crucible); The Americans (Arcola); Talking
Heads (Theatre Royal, York); Death of a
Salesman (Compass); The Norman Conquests
(Clwyd); Hobson's Choice (Lyric/West End);
Taming of the Shrew, The Winter's Tale, School
of Night, The Comedy of Errors, The Seagull,
A Midsummer Night's Dream, Epicoene or The
Silent Women, Dr Faustus, The Dillen,
Mary After the Queen, The Merry Wives of
Windsor, Il Candelaio, The Crucible (RSC);
The Public (Stratford East); A Chorus Line
(Drury Lane).
Television includes: Blair, The Battle of the Bible,
The Bill, Dalzeil & Pascoe, Murder in Mind,
Doctors, Bad Girls, Merseybeat, Holby City,
The Savages, The Infinite Worlds of H G Wells,
Baddiel's Syndrome, Pretending To Be Judith,
Where the Heart Is, Mind Games, Dinner
Ladies, 10th Kingdom, Mystery of Men, Close
Relations, Midsomer Murders, McCallum,
Insiders, A Touch of Frost, Peak Practice,
Wide Eyed and Legless, Casualty, The Devil's
Disciple, The Prisoner of Zenda, The Long and
The Short and The Tall, Sweet As You Are,
The Good Companions, Spearhead, Out or Not,
Out of the Blue.
Film includes: And When Did You Last See Your
Father, Love Me Still, If Only, Little Voice,
Fast Food.

Katharina Wienecke (assistant director)

As director, theatre includes: High Fidelity
(Deutsches Schauspielhaus, Hamburg).
As assistant director, theatre includes:
La Bohème (Garden Opera Co.); Othello,
Woyzeck, The Show Must Go On, Macbeth,
Offending the Audience, The Three Sisters,
Studio Braun (Deutsches Schauspielhaus,
Hamburg); A Midsummer Night's Dream
(Theater Freiburg); hamlet_X (Volksbühne am
Rosa-Luxemburg-Platz, Berlin); The Night Before
the Forests, Time and the Room, King Lear
(Deutsches Theater, Berlin); LEMonSPACE II
(Pavillion am Weinberg, Berlin).
Katharina is a member of Genesis Young
Director's Project at Young Vic.

Anthony Ward (designer)

For the Royal Court: Rhinoceros.
Other theatre includes: Macbeth (Gielgud/
Chichester Festival); Dying City (Lincoln Centre,
New York); Chitty Chitty Bang Bang (London
Palladium/Broadway); Gypsy (Broadway);
Nutcracker! (Sadler's Wells/UK tour); Oliver!
(London Palladium); Napoli Milionaria, Sweet
Bird of Youth, John Gabriel Borkman, The Way of
the World, La Grande Magia, Othello,
The Invention of Love, My Fair Lady, Oklahoma!,
The Royal Hunt of the Sun (National);
A Midsummer Night's Dream,
King Lear, The Tempest, Artists and Admirers,
The Winter's Tale, The Alchemist, The Virtuoso,
Troilus and Cressida, Cymbeline, Twelfth Night,
The Lion the Witch and the Wardrobe (RSC);
Twelfth Night (Donmar/Brooklyn Academy of
Music); Uncle Vanya, Assassins, Nine, To The
Green Fields Beyond (Donmar); Mary Stuart
(Donmar/Apollo); The Rehearsal, Dona Rosita,
The Novice (Almeida).
Opera includes: The Makropulos Case
(Metropolitan Opera NY); L'Etoile, Yollnde,
La Boheme, Peter Grimes & Gloriana (Opera
North); Macbeth (ROH); Manon Lescaut
(ROH/Paris Opera); Il ritorno d'Ulisse in patria
(Festival d'Aix-en-Provence).
Ballet includes: Masquerade, Les Rendez-vous,
Dance Variations (Royal Ballet).
Awards include: 2005 Outer Critics' Circle Set
Design Award for Chitty Chitty Bang Bang; 2003
OBIE Award for Uncle Vanya; 2002 Outer
Crictics' Circle Best Scenic Design Award for
Oklahoma!; 1999 Olivier Award for Costume
Design for A Midsummer Night's Dream,
La Grande Magia and The Way of the World;
1996 Olivier Award for Set Design for
Oklahoma!.

THE ENGLISH STAGE COMPANY
AT THE ROYAL COURT

'For me the theatre is really a religion or way of life. You must decide what you feel the world is about and what you want to say about it, so that everything in the theatre you work in is saying the same thing … A theatre must have a recognisable attitude. It will have one, whether you like it or not.'

George Devine, first artistic director of the English Stage Company: notes for an unwritten book.

The Royal Court Theatre in London's Sloane Square has presented some of the most influential plays in modern theatre history. At the turn of the twentieth century, the Royal Court was under the direction of Harley Granville-Barker and staged plays by Ibsen, Galsworthy, Yeats, Maeterlinck and Shaw. In 1956 George Devine became the first Artistic Director of the English Stage Company at the Royal Court. His intention was to create an international theatre of experiment that was devoted to the discovery of the future in playwriting. The production of John Osborne's Look Back in Anger in 1956 ushered in a new generation of playwrights, directors, actors and designers who together established the Court as the first theatre in London that prioritised the work of contemporary playwrights. Among them were Arnold Wesker, Ann Jellicoe, Edward Bond, John Arden, Christopher Hampton and David Storey. New plays were programmed alongside classics, and the company was from its earliest days committed to producing the best new international plays, including those of Ionesco, Genet and Beckett.

In 1969 the Royal Court opened the first second space in a British theatre; the Jerwood Theatre Upstairs has been a site for radical experimentation and has introduced audiences to some of the most influential new voices of the last 40 years, including Wole Soyinka, Caryl Churchill, David Hare, Howard Brenton, Howard Barker, Peter Gill, Martin Crimp, Sam Shepard and Jim Cartwright. Many outstanding young playwrights have established their careers here; among them Joe Penhall, Sarah Kane, Roy Williams, Rebecca Prichard, Mark Ravenhill, Martin McDonagh, Conor McPherson, Simon Stephens and debbie tucker green.

The Royal Court's Artistic Programme is only partially about the work seen on its stages. Many of its resources, and indeed the roots of the organisation, are devoted to the discovery and nurturing of new writers and the development of new plays. The Royal Court is in the business of asking questions about the world we live in and about what a play itself can be. The theatre's aim is to support both new and established writers in exploring new territory.

The Royal Court has a rich and productive infrastructure for the discovery and development of playwrights:

photo: Stephen Cummiiskey

International Programme
Since 1992 the Royal Court has initiated and developed lasting relationships with international playwrights and theatre practitioners. Creative dialogue is ongoing with theatre practitioners from many countries, including Brazil, Cuba, France, Germany, India, Mexico, Nigeria, Palestine, Russia, Spain and Syria. Many of the world's most promising and exciting playwrights have presented their plays on the stages of the Royal Court, among them Marcos Barbosa, Roland Schimmelpfennig, Marius von Mayenburg, Vassily Sigarev, the Presnyakov brothers and David Gieselmann. All of these influential projects are generously supported by the Genesis Foundation and the British Council.

The Young Writers Programme
Our Young Writers Programme seeks to open up theatre to the most exciting and diverse range of new voices around today, encouraging and inspiring young writers to use the theatre as a means of exploring their world, and helping them to flourish as artists. Week-long intensive playwriting projects for the 13-16 and 16-19 age groups are run during school holidays and each season playwriting groups for the 18-25 age group are led by our resident playwriting tutor Leo Butler.

Rough Cuts
The Royal Court's plays have frequently challenged the artistic, social and political orthodoxy of the day, pushing back the boundaries of what was acceptable or possible. That tradition of experiment and provocation has been intensified in the Rough Cuts seasons of experimental collaborations between playwrights and other artists, which are presented as raw and immediate works-in-progress in the Jerwood Theatre Upstairs.

The Royal Court's long and successful history of innovation has been built by generations of gifted and imaginative individuals. For information on the many exciting ways you can help support the theatre, please contact the Development Department on 020 7565 5079.

PROGRAMME SUPPORTERS

The Royal Court (English Stage Company Ltd) receives its principal funding from Arts Council England, London. It is also supported financially by a wide range of private companies, charitable and public bodies, and earns the remainder of its income from the box office and its own trading activities.

The Genesis Foundation supports the Royal Court's work with International Playwrights.

The Jerwood Charity supports new plays by new playwrights through the Jerwood New Playwrights series.

The Artistic Director's Chair is supported by a lead grant from The Peter Jay Sharp Foundation, contributing to the activities of the Artistic Director's office. Over the past ten years the BBC has supported the Gerald Chapman Fund for directors.

American Friends of the Royal Court are primarily focused on raising funds to enable the theatre to produce new work by emerging American writers. AFRCT has also supported the participation of young artists in the Royal Court's acclaimed International Residency. Contact: 001-212-946-5724.

ROYAL COURT
DEVELOPMENT BOARD
John Ayton
Anthony Burton
Sindy Caplan (Vice-Chair)
Gavin Casey FCA
Cas Donald
Allie Esiri
AC Farstad
Celeste Fenichel
Emma Marsh
Gavin Neath
Mark Robinson
William Russell (Chair)

PUBLIC FUNDING
Arts Council England,
London
British Council
London Challenge
Royal Borough of
Kensington & Chelsea

TRUSTS AND
FOUNDATIONS
American Friends of the
Royal Court Theatre
Bulldog Prinsep Theatrical
Fund
Gerald Chapman Fund
Columbia Foundation
The Sidney & Elizabeth
Corob Charitable Trust
Cowley Charitable Trust
The Dorset Foundation
The D'oyly Carte
Charitable Trust
The Ronald Duncan
Literary Foundation
The Edwin Fox
Foundation
The Foyle Foundation
Francis Finlay
The Garfield Weston
Foundation
Genesis Foundation
Haberdashers' Company
Sheila Hancock
Jerwood Charity
Lloyds TSB Foundation for
England and Wales
Dorothy Loudon
Foundation
Lynn Foundation

John Lyon's Charity
The Magowan Family
Foundation
The Laura Pels
Foundation
The Martin Bowley
Charitable Trust
Paul Hamlyn Foundation
The Peggy Ramsay
Foundation
Quercus Charitable Trust
Rose Foundation
Royal College of
Psychiatrists
The Royal Victoria Hall
Foundation
The Peter Jay Sharp
Foundation
Sobell Foundation
Wates Foundation

SPONSORS
Arts & Business
BBC
Coutts & Co
Dom Perignon
Kudos Film and Television
Links of London
Pemberton Greenish
Smythson of Bond Street

BUSINESS BENEFACTORS &
MEMBERS
Grey London
Hugo Boss
Lazard
Merrill Lynch
Tiffany & Co.
Vanity Fair

PRODUCTION SYNDICATE
Anonymous
Dianne & Michael Bienes
Ms Kay Ellen Consolver
Mrs Philip Donald
Daniel & Joanna Friel
John Garfield
Peter & Edna Goldstein
Miles Morland
Daisy Prince
William & Hilary Russell
Jon & NoraLee Sedmak
Ian & Carol Sellars

INDIVIDUAL MEMBERS
Patrons
Anonymous
Katie Bradford
Simon & Karen Day
Cas Donald
Tom & Simone Fenton
Tim Fosberry
John Garfield
Nick Gould
Sue & Don Guiney
Richard & Marcia Grand
Charles & Elizabeth
Handy
Jan Harris
Jack & Linda Keenan
Pawel & Sarah Kisielewski
Kathryn Ludlow
Deborah & Stephen
Marquardt
Duncan Matthews QC
Miles Morland
Jill & Paul Ruddock
William & Hilary Russell
Ian & Carol Sellars
Jan & Michael Topham

Benefactors
Anonymous
Martha Allfrey
Amanda Attard-Manché
Jane Attias
Varian Ayers & Gary
Knisely
John & Anoushka Ayton
Mr & Mrs Gavin Casey
Sindy & Jonathan Caplan
Jeremy Conway & Nicola
Van Gelder
Robyn Durie
Hugo Eddis
Joachim Fleury
Beverley Gee
Lydia & Manfred Gorvy
Claire Guinness
Sam & Caroline Haubold
The Hon. Mrs George Iliffe
Nicholas Josefowitz
David Kaskell &
Christopher Teano
Peter & Maria Kellner
Colette & Peter Levy

Larry & Peggy Levy
Emma Marsh
Barbara Minto
Pat Morton
Elaine Potter
Kadee Robbins
Mark Robinson
Lois Sieff OBE
Brian D Smith
Sue Stapely
Carl & Martha Tack
Amanda Vail

Associates
Anonymous
Cynthia Corbett
Andrew Cryer
Shantelle David
Kim Dunn
Celeste Fenichel
Charlotte & Nick Fraser
Gillian Frumkin
Julia Fuller
Sara Galbraith &
Robert Ham
Linda Grosse
David Lanch
Lady Lever
Mr Watcyn Lewis
Annie Macdonald
David Marks
Robert & Nicola
McFarland
Gavin & Ann Neath
Janet & Michael Orr
Pauline Pinder
William Poeton CBE &
Barbara Poeton
Jenny Sheridan
Gail Steele
Nick Steidl
Silke Ziehl

FOR THE ROYAL COURT

ENGLISH STAGE COMPANY

The Arsonists

A moral play without a moral

Characters

Gottlieb Biedermann
Babette, *his wife*
Anna, *a maidservant*
Schmitz, *a wrestler*
Eisenring, *a waiter*
Policeman
Mrs Knechtling
Doctor of Philosophy
Firemen's Leader
Chorus of Firemen

Settings

A living room
An attic

Prologue

The stage is dark, then we see **Biedermann**'s *face as he lights a cigarette. Immediately he has lit it,* **Firemen** *in helmets appear threateningly all around him.*

Biedermann   It's not easy these days, lighting a cigarette.

Pause.

Everyone thinks the whole world's about to go up in flames.

Pause.

Don't you just hate it?

Biedermann *hides the lit cigarette and slips away, whereupon the* **Firemen** *step forward in the manner of a Greek chorus.*

A church clock strikes a quarter past the hour.

Chorus
Citizens of this town
Observe us, the guardians of this town,
Watching
Listening
Always well disposed
Towards the well-disposed citizen.

Leader
Who in the end pays our wages.

Chorus
Our equipment all gleaming,
We circle your home
Watchful
Yet never thinking the worst.

Leader
Sometimes we stop,
Take the weight off our feet,
But never in order to sleep.
We are untiring.

Chorus
> Watching
> Listening
> So the combustible threat
> Hidden from sight
> Is revealed
> Before it's too late
> To put out the flames.

The church clock strikes the half-hour.

Leader
> Many things burn
> But not every fire
> Is determined by fate.
> Sometimes the fire
> Can be prevented.

Chorus
> It's only human
> To talk about fate.
> Fate means we don't need to ask
> Why the city is burning
> No need to ask how the terror began.

Leader
> It's only human,

Chorus
> It's all too human,

Leader
> To wipe out a few human beings.

The church clock strikes three-quarters.

Chorus
> Reason can save us from evil.

Leader
> That's right.

Chorus
> It's unworthy of God

And unworthy of man
If the nonsense that happens
Is put down to fate
Just because it has happened.

If humans start thinking like that
Then they will not deserve
Their place on this earth
This generous earth
That is fruitful and gracious to man.
They will not deserve
Their place in the sun
They will not deserve
The air that they breathe.

If the nonsense that happens
Is put down to fate
Just because it has happened
Then the flames may rise
To the point where nobody knows
How to put out the fire.

Leader

Our watch has begun.

The **Chorus** *sits down, while the clock strikes nine.*

Scene One

Living room.

Gottlieb Biedermann *is sitting in his living room, reading the newspaper and smoking a cigarette.* **Anna**, *the maidservant, wearing a little white apron, brings a bottle of wine.*

Anna   Mr Biedermann?

No reply.

Mr Biedermann –

He folds the newspaper up.

Biedermann   Firebombers again. They should hang the lot of them. I've said it before and I'll say it again. Hang the lot of them. It's the same story every time: someone at the door trying to sell you something, ends up being invited in. Wangles his way into staying overnight. Gets offered a corner of the attic to sleep in. Incredible . . .

He takes the bottle.

They should hang the lot of them!

He takes the corkscrew.

Anna   Mr Biedermann –

Biedermann   What is it?

Anna   He's still there.

Biedermann   Who's still there?

Anna   The man waiting in the hall. He wants to speak to you.

Biedermann   Say I'm not at home.

Anna   I told him that, Mr Biedermann, I told him that about an hour ago. He says he knows you. I can't throw him out on the street, sir, I just can't.

Biedermann   Why not?

Anna   He's too big.

Biedermann *uncorks the bottle.*

Biedermann   Tell him to come to my office tomorrow.

Anna   I've told him that at least three times, Mr Biedermann, but he's not interested in coming to your office.

Biedermann   Why not?

Anna   He says he doesn't want any of your hair rejuvenator.

Biedermann   What does he want then?

Anna   A little humanity.

Biedermann *sniffs at the cork.*

Biedermann   Tell him to clear off right now, or I'll throw him out myself.

He carefully pours wine into his burgundy glass.

A little humanity . . .

He tastes the wine.

He can wait in the hall. I'll be there in a minute. I'm not insensitive, but . . . I'm not insensitive, Anna, you know that, but I won't let strangers into the house. If I've told you once, I've told you a hundred times. Even if we had *three* spare beds, it still wouldn't be on. I'm sorry, it's just not on. You know what that leads to – these days . . .

Anna *makes to leave, but sees that* **Schmitz** *has just entered. He is athletic, his clothing half reminiscent of prison and half reminiscent of the circus. He has a tattoo on one arm, leather cuffs round his wrists.* **Anna** *slips out.* **Schmitz** *waits till* **Biedermann** *has tasted his wine and turned round.*

Schmitz   Good evening.

An astonished **Biedermann** *drops his cigar.*

Schmitz   Your cigar, Mr Biedermann.

He picks up the cigar and gives it to **Biedermann**

Biedermann   Now wait a minute –

Schmitz   Good evening!

Biedermann   What's going on? I told my maid very clearly that you were to wait in the hall. How – well, I mean . . . you didn't even knock . . .

Schmitz   My name is Schmitz.

Biedermann   You didn't even knock.

Schmitz   Josef Schmitz.

Silence.

Good evening!

Biedermann   What is it you want?

Schmitz   No cause for alarm, Mr Biedermann. I'm not trying to sell you anything.

Biedermann   Who are you then?

Schmitz   Wrestler by profession,

Biedermann   Wrestler?

Schmitz   Heavyweight.

Biedermann   I see.

Schmitz   Well, used to be a wrestler.

Biedermann   And now?

Schmitz   Unemployed.

Pause.

No cause for alarm, Mr Biedermann. I'm not looking for work. Not wrestling work, anyway. I've gone off wrestling . . . Only came here to get out of the rain.

Pause.

It's warmer in here.

Pause.

I hope I'm not disturbing you?

Pause.

Biedermann   Do you smoke?

He offers cigars.

Schmitz   You don't know what it's like for me, Mr Biedermann, being this big. Everybody's afraid of me . . . Thanks.

Biedermann *gives him a light.*

Schmitz   Thanks.

They stand and smoke.

Biedermann   I'll come straight to the point. What do you want?

Schmitz   My name is Schmitz.

Biedermann   So you said. Lovely to meet you, but −

Schmitz   I'm homeless.

He savours the cigar.

I'm homeless.

Biedermann   Would you like − some bread?

Schmitz   If that's all you have . . .

Biedermann   Or a glass of wine?

Schmitz   Ah, the bread and the wine . . . But not if I'm disturbing you, Mr Biedermann, not if I'm disturbing you.

Biedermann *goes to the door.*

Biedermann   Anna!

He comes back.

Schmitz   That girl said you were going to throw me out. But I thought, no, I thought, Mr Biedermann wouldn't do a thing like that.

Anna *has entered.*

Biedermann   Anna, bring another glass.

Anna   Yes, Mr Biedermann.

Biedermann   Oh, yes, and some bread −

Schmitz   And if it's no trouble to the young lady, some butter. And some cheese, and perhaps a little cold meat. Something along those lines. But don't put yourself out. Oh, and a few gherkins, and maybe a tomato. And a little mustard. Just whatever you happen to have.

Anna   I'll see what I can do.

Schmitz   But don't put yourself out.

Anna *leaves.*

Biedermann   You told her you knew me.

Schmitz   Indeed I do, Mr Biedermann, indeed I do.

Biedermann   Where from?

Schmitz   Only from your good side, Mr Biedermann. Yes, I have seen your good side.

Biedermann   Oh?

Schmitz   Last night in the café, at your usual table. You wouldn't have seen me, I was in the corner. I must say, we all loved it every time you banged your fist.

Biedermann   What was I saying?

Schmitz   The right thing.

He smokes his cigarette, then:

They should hang the lot of them. Every last one. The sooner the better. String them up. The arsonists, I mean.

Biedermann *offers him a seat.*

Biedermann   Please –

Schmitz *sits down.*

Schmitz   Men like you, Mr Biedermann, that's exactly what we need.

Biedermann   Yes, that's true of course, but –

Schmitz   No buts, Mr Biedermann. No buts. They don't make them like you any more. You still have a positive attitude. It follows.

Biedermann   True –

Schmitz   You still have civic courage.

Biedermann   Yes –

Schmitz   You see? It follows.

Biedermann   Yes. What follows?

Schmitz   Well, you still have a conscience. As everyone in that café could tell. A genuine conscience.

Biedermann   Well, yes, naturally, I –

Schmitz   But it's not natural, Mr Biedermann. Not these days. Take the circus where I used to work as a wrestler – the one that got burnt down – my boss there, if I ever mentioned conscience, he used to say, you must be joking. You must be joking, he used to say. Joe, he would say – that's short for Josef – Joe, he would say, what do I need a conscience for? That's what he would say, straight out. For circus animals I need a whip, not a conscience, he'd say. That's the sort of man he was. A conscience, he'd always say, don't make me laugh. If anyone has a conscience, it's normally a bad conscience. That's what he'd say.

He relishes the cigar.

May he rest in peace.

Biedermann   He's dead?

Schmitz   Burnt to death. Along with everything he owned.

A grandfather clock strikes nine.

Biedermann   I don't know why that girl's taking so long.

Schmitz   I'm not in a hurry –

They suddenly happen to look one another in the eye.

And you don't have a spare bed. As the maid explained.

Biedermann   Why are you laughing?

Schmitz   'No spare bed, unfortunately.' You see, that's what they all say. The minute a homeless man comes to the door and – not that I'm asking for a bed.

Biedermann   No?

Schmitz   I'm used to sleeping on the floor, Mr Biedermann. My father was a miner, you see. I'm used to it . . .

He blows the smoke out.

No buts, Mr Biedermann, no buts. You're not one of those
men who talk big to hide how scared they are. Not you, Mr
Biedermann. 'No spare bed, unfortunately.' As they all say. But
you, Mr Biedermann, I take your word for it. I believe you.
Where will it all end if we stop believing one another? That's
what I say, where will it all end, eh? Everybody thinking the
other bloke is an arsonist. Nothing but mutual suspicion in
the world. Am I right? Yesterday the whole café could tell that
you still believe in the goodness of people, not to mention the
goodness within yourself. Am I right? You're the first person
in this town who doesn't treat me as if I'm no better than an
arsonist.

Biedermann   Have an ashtray.

Schmitz   Am I right?

He carefully flicks ash into the ashtray.

These days most people don't believe in God. They believe in
the fire brigade.

Biedermann   What do you mean by that?

Schmitz   The truth.

Anna *enters with a tray.*

Anna   There's no cold meat.

Schmitz   That's all right, darling, there's enough there. (*Beat.*)
You forgot the mustard.

Anna   I'm sorry.

She leaves.

Biedermann   Eat up!

He fills their glasses.

Schmitz   You don't get this kind of welcome just anywhere
these days, you know. The things I've seen . . . People like me,
no suit to wear, no place to live, nothing to eat, we're hardly

through the door and it's 'Do take a seat' while behind your
back they're calling the police. What do you think of that, eh?
I ask for a place to stay, nothing more, me a decent, well-behaved
wrestler, who's wrestled for years, then some well-dressed bloke
who's never wrestled in his life grabs me by the scruff of the
neck . . . What's that for? I ask, and all I do is turn round so I
can look him in the face and – and, oh dear, look, he's acquired
a dislocated shoulder.

He takes the glass.

Cheers!

They drink, and **Schmitz** *begins to eat.*

Biedermann   I'll tell you what it's like these days. You open
a newspaper and there you are, another house burnt down.
And it's always the same old story, it's incredible. A complete
stranger comes to the door, asks for a bed for the night, and
the next day the house is in flames. What I mean is, well, to be
perfectly frank, a certain degree of mistrust is understandable.

He reaches for his newspaper.

Take a look for yourself.

He lays the open newspaper beside **Schmitz***'s plate.*

Schmitz   I've seen it.

Biedermann   An entire district.

He gets up from his chair to show it to **Schmitz***.*

Biedermann   Go on. Read it.

Schmitz *eats and drinks and reads.*

Schmitz   Is this a Beaujolais?

Biedermann   Yes.

Schmitz   Could be a little warmer . . .

Across his plate, he reads the paper.

'The fire appears to have been planned in exactly the same
way as last time.'

They look at one another.

Biedermann   It's incredible, isn't it?

Schmitz (*putting newspaper aside*)   That's why I don't read newspapers.

Biedermann   How do you mean?

Schmitz   It's always the same old stuff.

Biedermann   Yes, yes, I can see that, of course, but it's no solution, is it, just not reading the papers? At the end of the day, you have to know what you're up against.

Schmitz   Why?

Biedermann   You just have to.

Schmitz   Won't stop it happening.

He sniffs at the sausage.

It's God's judgement.

He cuts himself some sausage.

Biedermann   Do you think so?

Anna *brings the mustard.*

Schmitz   Thank you, darling, thank you.

Anna   Anything else?

Schmitz   Not today.

Anna *stops by the door.*

Schmitz   I love mustard. It's my favourite.

He squeezes mustard from the tube.

Biedermann   Why's it God's judgement?

Schmitz   How should I know?

He eats, and looks at the newspaper again.

'According to experts, the fire appears to have been planned in exactly the same way as last time.'

He laughs briefly, then fills his glass with wine.

Anna   Mr Biedermann?

Biedermann   What is it?

Anna   Mr Knechtling would like to speak to you.

Biedermann   Knechtling? Now? Knechtling?

Anna   He says –

Biedermann   It's not possible now.

Anna   He says he can't understand why you –

Biedermann   What does he need to understand?

Anna   Apparently he has a sick wife and three children.

Biedermann   No, it's completely out of the question.

He stands up impatiently.

Mr Knechtling! Mr Knechtling! Bloody hell. Either Mr
Knechtling can leave me alone, or he can go and find himself
a lawyer. Anyway, it's outside office hours. Mr Knechtling!
I'm not putting up with this behaviour just because a man's
lost his job. It's ridiculous. And there is social security, in case
he hasn't noticed. Better benefits than ever before . . . Yes, he
can go and talk to a lawyer, and I'll do the same. A share of
the profits from his invention! What a load of rubbish. He can
go and stick his head in an oven or find himself a lawyer,
whichever he prefers. If he can afford a lawyer. But if that's
what he wants, fine, he can go right ahead.

He looks at **Schmitz** *and regains control.*

Biedermann   Tell him I have a visitor.

Anna *leaves.*

Biedermann   I'm so sorry.

Schmitz   You're in your own home, Mr Biedermann.

Biedermann   How's the food?

He sits down and watches his guest enjoy the food.

Schmitz   Who would have thought it, eh? Who'd have thought you'd still find something like this?

Biedermann   Mustard?

Schmitz   Humanity.

He puts the cap back on the tube of mustard.

All I mean is, you're not grabbing me by the scruff of the neck and throwing me out on the street, out in the rain, now are you? You see, that's what we need, Mr Biedermann, a little humanity.

He takes the bottle and pours himself some wine.

God bless.

He drinks, obviously enjoying it.

Biedermann   I don't want you to think I'm insensitive . . .

Schmitz   Mr Biedermann!

Biedermann   That's what Mrs Knechtling is saying, you see.

Schmitz   If you were insensitive, you wouldn't be offering me a bed for the night, now would you?

Biedermann   That's true.

Schmitz   Even if it's only a corner of the attic.

He puts down his glass.

The wine's about right now.

The doorbell rings.

Schmitz   Police?

Biedermann   My wife.

Schmitz   Oh.

The bell rings again.

Biedermann   Come on. But on one condition. Not a sound out of you. My wife has a heart complaint.

We hear women's voices outside. **Biedermann** *gestures to* **Schmitz** *to hurry up, and helps clear away the tray, glass and bottle, which they take with them as they tiptoe off left, where the* **Chorus** *is sitting.*

Biedermann   Excuse me.

He climbs over the bench on which the **Chorus** *is sitting.*

Biedermann   Excuse me.

They leave, while **Babette** *enters from the right, accompanied by* **Anna**, *who takes her things from her.*

Babette   Where's my husband? You know, Anna, we're not narrow-minded. You can have a boyfriend, but I don't want you sneaking him into the house.

Anna   Mrs Biedermann, I don't have a boyfriend.

Babette   Then whose is that bike outside the front door? It scared me to death –

Attic.

Biedermann *snaps the light on. We see the loft space. He waves to* **Schmitz** *to come in. They talk in a whisper.*

Biedermann   The switch is here . . . If you're cold, there's an old sheepskin jacket somewhere, I think . . . Keep it quiet, for God's sake! . . . Take your shoes off!

Schmitz *puts the tray down and takes one shoe off.*

Biedermann   Mr Schmitz –

Schmitz   Mr Biedermann?

Biedermann   You promise me, you're really not an arsonist?

Schmitz *laughs.*

Biedermann   Shhh!

He nods goodnight, goes out and closes the door. **Schmitz** *takes his other shoe off.*

Living room.

Babette, *crossing the stage, has heard something. She looks up, horrified. Then, suddenly relieved, she turns to the audience.*

Babette   Gottlieb – that's my husband – Gottlieb has promised me he'll personally check the attic on a nightly basis, to make sure there are no arsonists up there. I can't tell you how grateful I am. I mean, otherwise I wouldn't sleep a wink.

Attic.

Schmitz, *now in socks, goes to the light switch and puts the light out.*

Chorus
> Citizens of this town,
> See how we watch over you,
> Guarding your innocence.
> Still watchful
> Yet still not thinking the worst,
> Well disposed towards the slumbering town,
> Sitting,
> Standing –

Leader
> Sometimes lighting a roll-up to help pass the time.

Chorus
> Watching
> Listening
> To make sure no flames
> Burst out through the roofs
> And lay waste to our town.

A clock tower strikes three.

Leader
> Everyone knows we're here,
> Just give us a shout.

He rolls his cigarette.

Chorus
> Who's switching on lights

In the downstairs rooms
At this time of night?
It's Biedermann's wife,
A bundle of nerves,
Sleepless and wretched.

Babette *appears in a dressing gown.*

Babette   Somebody's coughing!

We hear snoring.

Gottlieb! Don't you hear it?

We hear coughing.

There's somebody there!

We hear snoring.

Men! First sign of trouble, what do they do? They take a
sleeping pill.

The clock tower strikes four.

Leader
    It's four o'clock.

Babette *puts the light out.*

Leader
    And nobody's called us.

He puts his roll-up away. In the background it grows light.

Chorus
    First rays of the sun,
    One blink of God's eye,
    The roofs appear,
    And it's daylight again.
    All hail the firefighters!
    The town has survived
    One more night.
    All hail the firefighters!

*The **Chorus** sits down.*

Scene Two

Living room.

Biedermann *is standing with coat and hat on, leather briefcase under his arm. He is drinking his morning coffee and talking to somebody offstage.*

Biedermann   For the last time. He is not an arsonist!

Babette *(off)*   How do you know?

Biedermann   I asked him. And anyway, can we please talk about something else for a change? It's driving me mad, you and your arsonists, on and on and on.

Babette *enters with a milk jug.*

Biedermann   It's driving me mad!

Babette   Don't shout at me.

Biedermann   I'm not shouting at you, I'm just shouting in general.

She pours milk into his coffee.

I have to leave the house.

He drinks his coffee, which is too hot.

Where's it going to get us if we start thinking everyone's an arsonist? You need to have a bit of faith in people, Babette, a bit of trust –

He looks at his watch.

Babette   I'm not having it, Gottlieb, I'm just not having it. You're too good-natured. You do what your heart tells you, while I have to lie awake worrying all night. I'll give him breakfast, but then I'm telling him to go.

Biedermann   Do that.

Babette   In a friendly sort of way. I don't want to hurt his feelings.

Biedermann   Fine.

He puts down his cup.

I have to see my lawyer.

He gives **Babette** *a routine kiss just as* **Schmitz** *appears, wearing a sheepskin jacket. They don't see him at first.*

Babette   Why did you fire Knechtling?

Biedermann   Because I didn't need him any more.

Babette   You were always so pleased with him.

Biedermann   That's exactly what he's trying to exploit. A share of the profits from his invention! He knows very well what our hair rejuvenator is. Follica Plus is not an invention, it's a marketing opportunity. Follica Plus! The men who use it might as well be rubbing piss into their scalps.

Babette   Gottlieb!

Biedermann   Well, it's the truth.

He makes sure he has everything he needs in his briefcase.

You're right, I'm too good-natured. Knechtling. I'll wring his bloody neck.

About to leave, he sees **Schmitz**.

Schmitz   Good morning, friends!

Biedermann   Mr Schmitz –

Schmitz *extends his hand.*

Schmitz   Please. Call me Joe.

Biedermann *does not offer his hand.*

Biedermann   My wife will speak to you, Mr Schmitz. I have to go, I'm afraid. But I wish you all the best.

He shakes **Schmitz***'s hand.*

Biedermann   All the best, Mr Schmitz, all the best!

He sets off.

Schmitz   All the best, Gottlieb, all the best.

Babette *stares at him.*

Schmitz   Your husband is called Gottlieb, isn't he?

Babette   How did you sleep?

Schmitz   Thank you, I was cold. But I took the liberty of borrowing a sheepskin jacket. Took me back to my youth. Oh yes, I'm used to the cold.

Babette   Your breakfast's ready.

Schmitz   Mrs Biedermann!

She indicates his chair.

I can't accept this!

She fills his cup.

Babette   You eat up now, Joe. You probably have a long journey in front of you.

Schmitz   Do I?

She indicates his chair again.

Babette   Would you like a soft-boiled egg?

Schmitz   Two, please.

Babette   Anna!

Schmitz   Ah, Mrs Biedermann, I really feel at home here. May I?

He sits down.

Anna *enters.*

Babette   Two soft-boiled eggs.

Anna   Very good.

Schmitz   Three and a half minutes.

Anna   Very good.

She makes to leave.

Schmitz   Anna!

Anna *stops at the door.*

Schmitz   Good morning!

Anna   Morning. (*Leaves.*)

Schmitz   The way that girl looks at me. My God. If it were up to her, I'd be out in the pouring rain.

Babette *pours coffee for him.*

Babette   Mr Schmitz –

Schmitz   Yes?

Babette   If I may be perfectly frank –

Schmitz   Mrs Biedermann. You're trembling.

Babette   Mr Schmitz –

Schmitz   Is there a problem?

Babette   Have some cheese.

Schmitz   Thank you.

Babette   Or some jam?

Schmitz   Thank you.

Babette   Or some honey?

Schmitz   Oh, it's one thing after another, with you, Mrs Biedermann, one thing after another!

He leans back in his chair, eats his bread and butter, ready to listen.

What is it?

Babette   To be perfectly frank, Mr Schmitz –

Schmitz   Please. Call me Joe.

Babette   To be perfectly frank –

Schmitz   You want to get rid of me?

Babette   No, Mr Schmitz, no! I wouldn't put it like that at all –

Schmitz   How would you put it?

He takes some cheese.

I love Emmental. It's my favourite.

He leans back, eats, ready to listen.

So you think I'm an arsonist?

Babette   No, don't get me wrong. What was it I said? The last thing I want to do is hurt your feelings, I assure you. You've got me all confused now. Nobody's saying anything about arsonists. I have no complaints about your behaviour, Mr Schmitz –

He puts down his cutlery.

Schmitz   I know: I have no table manners.

Babette   No, no, that's not what I'm saying.

Schmitz   A man who eats like a pig.

Babette   Nonsense.

Schmitz   That's what they always told me in the orphanage. Schmitz, they used to say, stop eating like a pig.

Babette *takes the pot, to pour more coffee.*

Babette   No, no, for heaven's sake, that's not what I meant at all.

Schmitz (*holding his hand over the cup*)   I'm leaving.

Babette   Mr Schmitz –

Schmitz   I'm leaving.

Babette   One more cup?

He shakes his head.

Half a cup?

He shakes his head.

You can't just leave like this, Mr Schmitz. I didn't mean to upset you. I never said you eat like a pig.

He gets up.

Have I upset you?

He folds up the napkin.

Schmitz   It's not your fault I have no table manners. My father was a miner. Why should someone like me have table manners? Hunger and cold, I know how to handle hunger and cold, but − with no education, Mrs Biedermann, no manners, no culture . . .

Babette   I understand.

Schmitz   I'm off.

Babette   Where will you go?

Schmitz   Out into the rain . . .

Babette   Oh, God.

Schmitz   I'm used to it.

Babette   Mr Schmitz . . . Please don't look at me like that . . . Your father was a miner, I quite understand. You probably had a terribly hard childhood.

Schmitz   No, not really.

He drops his gaze and counts on his fingers.

My mother didn't die until I was . . . seven.

He turns round and wipes his eyes.

Babette   Joe! − But, Joe . . .

Anna *comes with the boiled eggs.*

Anna   Anything else?

She gets no answer, and leaves.

Babette   I'm not sending you away, I never said I was sending you away. What did I say? Really, you've completely misunderstood. Oh, this is so terrible. What can I do to make you believe me?

After some hesitation, she takes him by the sleeve.

Come on, Joe, sit down and eat!

Schmitz *sits down at the table again.*

Babette   What kind of people do you think we are? I never noticed that you eat like a pig, honestly. And even if you do, Gottlieb and I don't care about appearances, we're just not like that.

He slices the top off the egg

Schmitz   God bless.

Babette   Salt?

He eats the egg

Schmitz   It's true. You haven't sent me away, absolutely not. I'm very sorry about the misunderstanding. Please forgive me . . .

Babette   Is the egg right for you?

Schmitz   A little too runny . . . Please forgive me.

He has finished the egg

So what were you about to say, earlier? Something about being perfectly frank . . .

Babette   Yes, what was I about to say?

Schmitz (*slicing the top off the second egg*)   God bless. Now, Billy, he always says that individual acts of kindness don't happen any more. There are no decent people any more, no human beings left. Kindness has become a function of the state. According to Billy. That's why the world's going down the pan.

He puts salt on his egg

I can't wait to see his face, when he gets given a breakfast like this. Yes, Billy's going to be over the moon.

The doorbell rings.

Maybe that's him now.

The doorbell rings.

Babette   Billy? Who's Billy?

Schmitz   He's a man of culture, you wait and see. He used to be a waiter at the Metropole. Before it was burnt down, of course.

Babette   Burnt down?

Schmitz   Head waiter.

Anna *enters.*

Babette   Who is it?

Anna   A gentleman.

Babette   What does he want?

Anna   He says he's from the insurance. Says he needs to do a safety check.

Babette *gets up.*

Anna   Though he's dressed like a waiter.

Babette *and* **Anna** *go out.* **Schmitz** *pours himself some coffee.*

Schmitz   Good old Billy.

Chorus
Now there are two
To arouse
Our suspicion.
Bicycles,
We wonder who they belong to . . .

Leader
One bike from yesterday
One from today.

Chorus

Woe unto us!

Leader

Again it is night
Again we keep watch.

A clock tower strikes.

Chorus

The timid see dangers
With no danger there.
They fear their own shadows.
Brave when it's only a rumour,
They stumble through life
Filled with fear,
Till one day the rumour
Walks in through the door.

The clock tower strikes.

Leader

How should I read it –
Those two not leaving the house?

The clock tower strikes.

Chorus

The timid are blind,
More blind than the blind.
Hoping the evil
Is not really evil,
They welcome the evil.
Defenceless, exhausted by fear,
They hope for the best . . .
Until it's too late.

The clock tower strikes.

Chorus

Woe unto us!

*The **Chorus** sits down.*

Scene Three

Attic.

Schmitz *is still in his wrestler's costume, and* **Eisenring** *has taken off his waiter's jacket and is only wearing trousers and a waistcoat. Together they are rolling oil drums into the loft. These are metal drums, the kind used to transport fuel. Both men have taken off their shoes and are rolling the drums as quietly as possible.*

Eisenring   Shhh!

Schmitz   What happens if he decides to call the police?

Eisenring   A bit further.

Schmitz   What will we do?

Eisenring   Slowly, slowly . . . Stop.

They have now rolled the final drum up against the drums already there in the shadows. **Eisenring** *wipes his hands on a rag.*

Eisenring   Why would he call the police?

Schmitz   Why wouldn't he?

Eisenring   Because he's guilty too.

We hear pigeons cooing.

Damn. It's getting light. Let's get some sleep.

He throws the rag away.

Every citizen is guilty, actually. Above a certain income. There's nothing to worry about.

There is a knocking at the bolted door.

Biedermann   Open the door! Open the door!

He bangs and shakes the door.

Eisenring   Doesn't quite sound like an invitation to breakfast, does it?

Biedermann   Open the door! Immediately!

Schmitz　He's never been like this before.

The banging and thumping gets louder. **Eisenring** *puts his waiter's jacket back on, unhurried but nimble. He adjusts his tie, dusts himself down, then opens the door. In comes* **Biedermann** *in his dressing gown, not noticing the newcomer standing behind the door.*

Biedermann　Mr Schmitz!

Schmitz　Good morning, Mr Biedermann, good morning. I hope that stupid rumbling noise didn't wake you.

Biedermann　Mr Schmitz!

Schmitz　I promise it won't happen again.

Biedermann　Get out of my house.

Pause.

I said: get out of my house.

Schmitz　When?

Biedermann　This instant.

Schmitz　Why?

Biedermann　Otherwise my wife will call the police. I can't stop her and I won't stop her.

Schmitz　Hmmm.

Biedermann　You heard. This instant.

Pause.

What are you waiting for?

Schmitz, *silent, takes his shoes.*

Biedermann　I don't want any discussion.

Schmitz　I'm not saying a word.

Biedermann　If you think there's no limit to what I'll put up with, just because you're a wrestler – well, my God, what a dreadful noise. All night long.

He points with outstretched arm to the door.

Get out! I'm telling you, get out!

Schmitz *calls across to* **Eisenring**.

Schmitz   He's never been like this before.

Biedermann *turns and is speechless.*

Eisenring   My name's Eisenring.

Biedermann   Why are you – ?

Eisenring   William Eisenring. Call me Billy.

Biedermann   Why . . . why are there suddenly two of you?

Schmitz *and* **Eisenring** *look at one another.*

Biedermann   Without even asking!

Eisenring   You see?

Biedermann   What's going on?

Eisenring   I told you, didn't I? You just don't do that sort of thing, Joe. You have no manners. Without even asking! What sort of way is that to behave – suddenly two of us, without even asking?

Biedermann   I'm really, really angry about this.

Eisenring   You see? He's really, really angry about this.

He turns to **Biedermann**.

Eisenring   I told him.

He turns to **Schmitz**.

Eisenring   I told you, didn't I?

Schmitz *is ashamed.*

Biedermann   What on earth do you think you're doing? At the end of the day, I'm the homeowner. I'm asking you: what do you think you're doing?

Pause.

Eisenring   Answer when the gentleman speaks to you!

Pause.

Schmitz   Well, you see, Billy is my friend.

Biedermann   Go on.

Schmitz   We went to school together. As children.

Biedermann   And?

Schmitz   So I thought . . .

Biedermann   You thought what?

Pause.

Eisenring   You didn't think at all!

He turns to **Biedermann**.

Eisenring   I understand completely. There's a time and a place for everything, but in the end –

He shouts at **Schmitz**.

Eisenring   Do you think a man who owns his own house should put up with this kind of behaviour?

He turns to **Biedermann**.

Eisenring   He didn't even ask you, is that right?

Biedermann   Never mentioned it.

Eisenring   Joe –

Biedermann   Never mentioned it.

Eisenring   And you're surprised when people throw you out on the street?

He shakes his head and laughs as if **Schmitz** *is an idiot.*

Biedermann   It's no laughing matter! I'm very serious about this. My wife has a heart condition –

Eisenring   You see?

Biedermann   She was awake half the night, with that awful noise. What on earth are you doing?

He looks around him.

What in God's name are those oil drums for?

Schmitz *and* **Eisenring** *stare into a corner without drums.*

Biedermann   No, here. Over here! What's this?

Knocks on one of the drums.

What is it?

Schmitz   It's an oil drum.

Biedermann   And where have the oil drums come from?

Schmitz   Do you know where they've come from, Billy?

Eisenring   They're imported. Says on them.

Biedermann   Now listen –

Eisenring   Somewhere.

Eisenring *and* **Schmitz** *look for the label.*

Biedermann   I don't believe this. What do you think you're doing? The attic filled with oil drums. Piled high. Look. They're piled high.

Eisenring   Yes. They are.

Biedermann   Well . . . why?

Eisenring   Joe got his figures wrong. Twelve metres by fifteen, you said, and in fact the whole attic can't be more than a hundred square metres. I think you'll understand I can't just leave my oil drums out on the street.

Biedermann   I don't understand a thing.

Schmitz *shows him a label.*

Schmitz   Here it is, Mr Biedermann, look, here's the label!

Biedermann   I don't believe this.

Schmitz   Here it is. Where they come from. Here.

Biedermann   I just don't believe it. (*Looks at the label.*)

Living room.

Anna *leads a* **Policeman** *into the living room.*

Anna   I'll call him.

She goes and the **Policeman** *waits.*

Attic.

Biedermann   *Petrol?*

Living room.

Anna *comes back.*

Anna   What was it about, officer?

Policeman   It's an official matter.

Anna *goes and the* **Policeman** *waits.*

Attic.

Biedermann   Is this true? Is it?

Eisenring   Is what true?

Biedermann   What it says on the label!

He shows them the label.

How stupid do you think I am? Honestly. Do you think I can't read?

They look at the label.

Well?

He laughs at the outrageousness of it all.

Petrol! All right, all right.

In the sombre tones of an investigating judge:

What is in these metal drums?

Eisenring   Petrol.

Biedermann   I'm not in the mood for jokes. I'm asking you for the last time: what is in these drums? You know as well as I do that an attic isn't the place to store petrol.

He runs a finger over a drum.

Here. Smell it.

He holds his finger under their noses.

Is that petrol or is it not petrol?

They sniff, then look at one another.

Answer me!

Eisenring   It's petrol.

Schmitz   It's petrol.

Eisenring *and* **Schmitz**   It's definitely petrol.

Biedermann   Are you mad? The whole attic full of petrol?

Schmitz   That's why we're not smoking.

Biedermann   Don't you know the papers are full of warnings about this sort of thing? What do you think you're doing? My wife will have a fit.

Eisenring   You see?

Biedermann   Will you stop saying that?!

Eisenring   You can't do that to a housewife, Joe. I know a thing or two about housewives –

Anna (*calling from the stairwell*)   Mr Biedermann! Mr Biedermann!

Biedermann *shuts the door.*

Biedermann   Mr Schmitz! Mr . . .

Eisenring   Eisenring.

Biedermann   If you don't get these drums out of the house right now – and I mean right now – then –

Eisenring   Then you'll call the police.

Biedermann   Yes.

Schmitz   You see?

Anna (*calls*)   Mr Biedermann!

Biedermann (*whispers*)   That's my last word on the matter!

Eisenring   Which word was that?

Biedermann   I am not having petrol in my attic! Do you understand?! I'm not having it!

Somebody knocks at the door.

Coming.

He opens the door to leave and the **Policeman** *enters.*

Policeman   Ah, here you are, Mr Biedermann, found you at last, sir. No need to come downstairs, I shan't take up much of your time.

Biedermann   Good morning!

Policeman   Good morning!

Eisenring   Morning . . .

Schmitz   Morning . . .

Schmitz *and* **Eisenring** *bow.*

Policeman   It's concerning an accident –

Biedermann   Oh my God.

Policeman   Occurring to an elderly gentleman. His wife claims he used to work for you. As an inventor. Last night the said gentleman put his head in a gas oven.

He checks his notepad.

Name of Knechtling, Johan . . . residing at Number Eleven, Steed Street.

He puts his notepad away.

Were you acquainted with the deceased?

Biedermann   I . . .

Policeman   Perhaps you would prefer to have this
conversation in private, sir?

Biedermann   Yes.

Policeman   After all, it's nothing to do with your employees.

Biedermann   Quite.

He remains standing in the doorway.

If anyone's looking for me, I'm with the police. Understood?
I'll be right back.

Schmitz *and* **Eisenring** *nod.*

Policeman   Mr Biedermann –

Biedermann   Let's go.

Policeman   What have you got in those drums?

Biedermann   Me?

Policeman   If I might ask.

Biedermann   Hair rejuvenator.

He looks at **Schmitz** *and* **Eisenring**.

Eisenring   Follica Plus.

Schmitz   Good news for men.

Eisenring   Follica Plus.

Schmitz   At last, the answer to baldness.

Eisenring   Follica Plus.

Schmitz   Hair today, hair tomorrow.

Eisenring *and* **Schmitz**   Follica Plus! Follica Plus! Follica
Plus!

The **Policeman** *laughs.*

Biedermann   Is he dead?

Biedermann *and the* **Policeman** *leave.*

Eisenring   What a nice man.

Schmitz   Didn't I tell you?

Eisenring   Nothing about breakfast, though.

Schmitz   He's never been like this before . . .

Eisenring *reaches into his trouser pocket.*

Eisenring   Have you got the detonator?

Schmitz *reaches into his trouser pocket.*

Schmitz   Never been like this before . . .

Chorus
> First rays of the sun,
> One blink of God's eye,
> Rooftops appear,
> And it's daylight again.

Leader
> Today as it was yesterday.

Chorus
> All hail the firefighters!

Leader
> The town has survived.

Chorus
> All hail the firefighters!

Leader
> The town has survived
> One more night.

Chorus
> All hail the firefighters!

Noise of traffic, hooting of horns, a tram.

Leader
> To overcome danger
> We need to be smart

And think about what we observe.
By staying alert
We'll see signs of disaster
And act in good time –
If we want to.

Chorus
And what if we don't?

Leader
In order to know
What dangers we face
We open our newspapers daily.
Each morning at breakfast
Appalled by distant events
We let others explain what is happening,
So we're never required
To think for ourselves.
Daily discovering
What happened yesterday
Far, far away,
We fail to see clearly
What's happening right now
Under our noses
Under our roofs.

Chorus
Unpublished.

Leader
Obvious.

Chorus
Outrageous.

Leader
Real.

Chorus
Not keen to look at it
Otherwise –

The **Leader** *interrupts with a gesture.*

Leader

He's coming.

The **Chorus** *swings round.*

Chorus

The town has survived one more night,
Today as it was yesterday.
Watch as the citizen
Shining and shaved
Dashes to work
Forgetting the imminent danger.

Biedermann *enters in coat and hat, briefcase under his arm.*

Biedermann   Taxi! . . . Taxi? . . . Taxi!

The **Chorus** *stands in his way.*

Biedermann   What's going on?

Chorus

Woe unto us.

Biedermann   What can I do for you?

Chorus

Woe unto us.

Biedermann   So you said.

Chorus

Woe unto us.

Biedermann   Why?

Leader

We've seen something highly suspicious
Something inflammable
You've seen it too.
What do we make of it?

Something inflammable
Up in the attic.
Drums of petrol
Up in the attic.

Biedermann (*shouting*) What's it got to do with you?!

Silence.

Let me through. – I need to see my lawyer. What do you want?
I'm innocent . . .

He is scared.

What is this? An interrogation?

He shows masterful certainty.

Just let me through, all right?

*The **Chorus** stands motionless.*

Chorus
>   The Chorus should not sit in judgement
>   On citizens ready to act.
>   It wouldn't be right.

Leader
>   Eyeing events from the sidelines,
>   The Chorus is quicker to grasp
>   The imminent danger.

Chorus
>   As choruses do, we draw near,
>   Politely posing our questions,
>   Powerless, watchful,
>   Showing concern,
>   Issuing warnings,
>   Bathed in cold sweat,
>   Till it's too late to put out the flames,
>   Till even the firefighters
>   Cannot put out the flames.

Biedermann *looks at his watch.*

Biedermann I'm in a hurry.

Chorus
>   Woe unto us.

Biedermann I really don't know what you want.

Leader

Allowing those drums full of petrol,
Biedermann, Biedermann,
What did you think they were for?

Biedermann   What were they for?

Leader

Knowing how easy it is
To send the whole world up in flames,
Biedermann, Biedermann,
What were you thinking?

Biedermann   Thinking? (*He scrutinises the* **Chorus**.) Now
listen, I'm a free citizen. I can think what I want. Why all these
questions? I have the right not to think anything at all. Quite
apart from which, what goes on under my own roof . . . Well,
let's face it, I own this house.

Chorus

Let the holy of holies be holy:
Property.
Who cares where that takes us?
Who cares if it leads
To flames that can't be extinguished,
Flames that will sear us and scorch us?
Let the holy of holies be holy.

Biedermann   Well –

Silence.

Why won't you let me through?

Silence.

You shouldn't always think the worst, you know. Where does
that get you? I just want a quiet life, that's all, and as far as
those two upstairs are concerned, quite apart from the fact that
I have other things on my mind at the moment –

Babette *enters in coat and hat.*

Biedermann   What are you doing here?

Babette   Am I interrupting?

Biedermann   Yes. I'm having a meeting with the Chorus.

Babette *nods to the* **Chorus**, *then whispers in* **Biedermann***'s ear.*

Biedermann   With a ribbon, yes. A wreath with a ribbon. It doesn't matter what it costs.

Babette (*nodding to the* **Chorus**)   Sorry to interrupt.

She goes away.

Biedermann   All right. I'll come straight to the point. I've had enough. You and your arsonists. I don't even want to meet my friends any more; it's all they ever talk about. In the end, I only have one life to live. If we assume that everyone is an arsonist, how are things ever going to get better? We need to have a little bit of trust, a little bit of goodwill. That's what I think. Not always seeing evil round the corner. Not everyone's an arsonist, for God's sake! That's what I think. A little bit of trust. A little –

Pause.

I can't live in fear all the time.

Pause.

Do you think I slept last night? I'm not stupid, you know. Petrol is petrol! I grappled with some very difficult thoughts. I climbed on to the table, so as to hear better. I even got up on top of the wardrobe and put my ear against the ceiling. I did! They were snoring! Snoring! I climbed on top of that wardrobe at least four times. Snoring away, they were, dead to the world. At one point I got so angry I went out on to the stairs in my pyjamas – believe it or not. I was just about to wake those two and throw them out on the street, with my own two hands, just like that. Along with their drums of petrol. Even if it was the middle of the night.

Chorus
    With your own two hands?

Biedermann   Yes.

Chorus
  Just like that?

Biedermann   Yes.

Chorus
  In the middle of the night?

Biedermann   I was just about to do it. I would have done
it if my wife hadn't appeared. She was worried I'd catch a
cold. But I was just about to do it, oh yes.

Out of embarrassment, he takes a cigar.

Leader
  What should I make of it this time?
  Biedermann just couldn't sleep.
  Did he never once think
  That a citizen's goodness might be abused?
  Doubt overcame him.
  Why should that be?

Biedermann *lights his cigar.*

Chorus
  It's hard for a citizen
  Brutal in business
  Who's otherwise kind and considerate,
  Always prepared to do good.

Leader
  When it suits him.

Chorus
  Hoping that good
  Will come from being good-natured.
  He makes a deadly mistake.

Biedermann   What do you mean by that?

Chorus
  The curious odour of petrol.

Biedermann (*sniffing*)   I don't smell it.

Chorus
Woe unto us.

Biedermann   I can't smell a thing.

Leader
He's already so used to the odour of evil.

Chorus
Woe unto us.

Biedermann   Can you please stop all this woe-unto-us stuff? It's pure defeatism.

A car beeps its horn.

Taxi! Taxi!

A car stops.

Excuse me.

He hurries off.

Chorus
Where to, citizen?

A car drives off.

Leader
Poor unfortunate Biedermann,
What's he got planned?
Fearful-audacious, he struck me, and pale.
Then ran off fearful-decisive –
What for?

A car beeps.

Chorus
So used to the odour of evil.

A car beeps in the distance.

Woe unto us.

Leader
Woe unto you.

The **Chorus** *steps back, apart from the* **Leader**, *who takes out his roll-up.*

Leader
  If the thought of radical change
  Scares you more than the thought of disaster,
  What can you do
  To stop the disaster?

He follows the **Chorus**.

Scene Four

Attic.

Eisenring *is alone, unwinding cord from a reel. As he does so, he whistles 'Lili Marlene'. He interrupts his whistling to lick his finger and stick it out through the skylight to check the wind.*

Living room.

Biedermann *enters, followed by* **Babette**. *Cigar in mouth, he takes his coat off and throws his briefcase down.*

Biedermann   Just do what I ask.

Babette   A goose?

Biedermann   A goose.

Cigar still in mouth, he takes his jacket off.

Babette   Why are you taking your jacket off?

Biedermann (*handing her the jacket*)   If I report them to the police, I know I'll be making enemies of them. What good's that going to do us? One spark could set the whole house ablaze. What good's that going to do us? Whereas, if I go up and invite them to supper – assuming they accept my invitation . . .

Babette   Then?

Biedermann   Then they'll be our friends.

He leaves.

Babette Just so you know, Anna, you can't have the night off. We're having guests. Set the table for four.

Attic.

Eisenring *is singing 'Lili Marlene' when* **Biedermann** *knocks at the door.*

Eisenring Come in!

He continues to sing but nobody enters.

Come in!

Biedermann *enters, in shirtsleeves.*

Eisenring Morning, Mr Biedermann.

Biedermann May I?

Eisenring How did you sleep?

Biedermann Badly, thank you.

Eisenring Me too. It's the weather. Wind's from the south.

He continues his work with the cord and the reel.

Biedermann I don't mean to disturb you.

Eisenring But please, Mr Biedermann, you're in your own home.

Biedermann I don't want to impose.

We hear the cooing of pigeons.

Where's our friend?

Eisenring Who, Joe? Off working. The lazy sod didn't want to go without breakfast. I sent him to get firelighters.

Biedermann Firelighters?!

Eisenring Firelighters. Just to be on the safe side.

Biedermann *laughs politely, as if at a rather feeble joke.*

Biedermann   Safe . . . ha, ha, ha, very good, yes . . . No, what I meant to say was, what I meant to say −

Eisenring   You want to throw us out again?

Biedermann   No, what happened was, in the middle of the night − I'd run out of sleeping pills, you see − I realised in the middle of the night that you've got no toilet up here.

Eisenring   That's all right. We do it through the skylight.

Biedermann   Whatever suits you. Yes, fine by me. I just couldn't stop worrying about it, all night long. Maybe you'd like to wash, or take a shower? Please feel free to use my bathroom. I've told Anna to put towels in there for you.

He looks at **Eisenring***.*

Biedermann   Why are you shaking your head?

Eisenring   Where did he put it?

Biedermann   What?

Eisenring   Have you seen a detonator anywhere?

He looks here and there.

Biedermann   A detonator?!

Eisenring   Don't you worry about the bathroom, Mr Biedermann, really don't worry. There wasn't a bathroom in prison either.

Biedermann   Prison?

Eisenring   I just got out. Didn't Joe tell you?

Biedermann   No.

Eisenring   Didn't even mention it?

Biedermann   No.

Eisenring   Terrible. All that man ever talks about is himself. There are people like that, you know. But in the end, what can you do with someone who's had such a tragic youth? Did you have a tragic youth, Mr Biedermann? Not that I did! I could have studied, you know. My father wanted me to go into the law.

He stands at the skylight and talks to the pigeons.

Prrrr! Prrrr! Prrrr!

Biedermann *lights another cigar.*

Biedermann   Mr Eisenring, I didn't sleep all night, to be absolutely honest. Is it really petrol in those drums?

Eisenring   Don't you trust us?

Biedermann   I'm only asking.

Eisenring   What kind of people do you think we are? To be absolutely honest.

Biedermann   I don't want you to feel I've got no sense of humour, but I must say, your jokes can be, well, a little bit . . . unusual.

Eisenring   It's something we're working on.

Biedermann   What is?

Eisenring   Our jokes. You see, comedy is the third-best tactic. The second-best tactic is sentimentality. You know, the stuff that Joe comes out with: miner's family, childhood poverty, orphanage, all that bollocks. But in my experience, the best, the most reliable tactic is still the naked truth. Because, funnily enough, nobody believes it.

Living room.

Anna *ushers in* **Mrs Knechtling**, *dressed in black.*

Anna   Take a seat.

Mrs Knechtling *sits down.*

Anna   But if you're Mrs Knechtling, you're wasting your time. Mr Biedermann's made it clear that he wants nothing to do with you.

Mrs Knechtling *gets up.*

Anna   Take a seat!

Mrs Knechtling *sits down.*

Anna   But don't get your hopes up.

Anna *leaves.*

Attic.

Eisenring *is making himself busy.* **Biedermann** *stands and smokes.*

Eisenring   Why's Joe taking so long? Firelighters aren't that hard to find. Let's hope he hasn't had his collar felt.

Biedermann   Had his collar felt?

Eisenring   What's so funny about that?

Biedermann   Expressions like that, you know, well, it's as if you're from another planet. Having your collar felt! I find that fascinating. You see, in my world, people don't often 'get their collars felt'.

Eisenring   Because, in your world, people don't steal firelighters. Obviously. It's a class thing.

Biedermann   Rubbish.

Eisenring   You're not trying to tell me that –

Biedermann   I don't believe in class. I'm a man of my time, you see, in case you hadn't noticed. In fact, what I really can't stand is the attitude of the socially disadvantaged themselves, because they go on about class more than anyone else does! These days we're all human beings, aren't we? Rich or poor, we're all human beings. Even the middle classes. You and I, we're both made of flesh and blood, aren't we? . . . I don't know whether you smoke . . .

He offers a cigar, but **Eisenring** *shakes his head.*

Biedermann   I'm not saying everybody should be the same. There will always be stupid people and clever people, thank heavens, but why can't we be friends? A little bit of goodwill, for God's sake, a little idealism, a little – then we'd all have a quiet life, rich and poor together, don't you think?

Eisenring   If I may be frank –

Biedermann   I'm all for that.

Eisenring   You won't take offence?

Biedermann   The franker the better.

Eisenring   You're quite sure?

Biedermann   Absolutely certain.

Eisenring   You really shouldn't smoke in here.

Biedermann, *shocked, puts out his cigarette.*

Eisenring   It's not for me to lay down the rules, I know. At the end of the day, this is your home, but you understand –

Biedermann   Of course I do!

Eisenring   There it is!

He picks up something off the floor, and blows on it to clean it, before attaching it to the cord, once again whistling 'Lili Marlene'.

Biedermann   I'm sorry, what is it you're doing all the time? If you don't mind my asking. And what's that?

Eisenring   That's the detonator.

Biedermann   – ?

Eisenring   And that's the fuse wire.

Biedermann   – ?

Eisenring   Joe says the latest detonators are even better. But they've not been issued to the army yet, so we can't steal them, and buying them's out of the question. Military hardware's terribly expensive. Everything has to be top quality, you see.

Biedermann   Fuse wire? You did say 'fuse wire'?

Eisenring   Detonating fuse wire.

He gives **Biedermann** *the end of the fuse wire.*

Eisenring   Would you be kind enough to hold the end? . . .
So I can measure it.

Biedermann *holds the fuse wire.*

Biedermann   Joking apart –

Eisenring   It won't take a minute.

He whistles 'Lili Marlene' while measuring out the fuse wire.

Thank you, Mr Biedermann. Thank you so much.

Biedermann *suddenly has to laugh.*

Biedermann   I'm not someone you can make a fool of, you
know. Definitely not. I must say, you rather take it for granted
that people will see the funny side. I'm not surprised you get
arrested from time to time. Not everybody's sense of humour
is as highly developed as mine, you know.

Eisenring   You have to find the right sort of people.

Biedermann   If I said people were fundamentally decent,
everyone I know would laugh in my face.

Eisenring   Ha.

Biedermann   Mind you, I donated a fair old whack to the
local fire brigade. I'm not saying how much.

Eisenring   Ha.

He lays out the fuse wire.

Don't worry. Come the big day, everybody's going to cop it.
Sense of humour or no sense of humour.

Biedermann, *sweating, sits down on an oil drum.*

Eisenring   What's the matter, Mr Biedermann? You've gone
all pale!

He claps him on the shoulder.

It's this smell, isn't it? Petrol. If you're not used to it . . . I'll
open the skylight.

He opens the door.

Biedermann   Thank you.

Anna (*calling up the stairs*)   Mr Biedermann! Mr Biedermann!

Eisenring   Not the police again?

Anna   Mr Biedermann!

Eisenring   It's a police state, that's what it is.

Anna   Mr Biedermann!

Biedermann   I'm coming! (*Whispers.*) Do you like goose?

Eisenring   Goose?

Biedermann   Goose. Yes, goose.

Eisenring   Me? Like goose? Why?

Biedermann   With chestnut stuffing.

Eisenring   And red cabbage?

Biedermann   Yes. What I'm trying to say is, me and my wife, well, mainly me – we thought, I just thought, if it would appeal to you . . . I don't want to force you . . . But if you would like to join us for a bite to eat, you and Mr Schmitz –

Eisenring   This evening?

Biedermann   Is tomorrow better?

Eisenring   Oh, I think we'll be gone by tomorrow. No, this evening. This evening would be perfect. Thank you very much.

Biedermann   Shall we say, seven o'clock?

Anna (*calling up the stairs*)   Mr Biedermann!

Biedermann (*shaking hands*)   It's a deal?

Eisenring   It's a deal.

Biedermann *makes to leave, but stops in the doorway, nodding agreeably while staring blankly at the drums and fuse wire.*

Eisenring   It's a deal.

Biedermann *leaves.* **Eisenring** *works on, whistling. Enter the* **Chorus**, *as if the scene were ended. But as the* **Chorus** *assembles downstage, there is a noise from above. Something has fallen over.*

Eisenring   You can come out now.

The **Doctor of Philosophy**, *wearing glasses, crawls out from between the oil drums.*

Eisenring   You heard: Joe and I have been invited downstairs for supper. You keep watch here. Make sure nobody comes in here and starts smoking. At least not yet. Got that?

The **Doctor** *polishes his spectacles.*

Eisenring   You know, sometimes I wonder why you're with us. You don't really enjoy it, do you, setting places on fire? You don't get off on it. The sparks, the flames, the smoke, the noise. Dogs barking, people screaming, fire engines arriving too late. Ashes. None of that does a thing for you, does it?

The **Doctor** *puts his spectacles on, silent and earnest.* **Eisenring** *laughs.*

Eisenring   Do-gooder!

He whistles a little without looking at the **Doctor**.

Eisenring   I don't much like academics. But you know that, Doctor, don't you? I told you that from the start. Academics like you don't get any kind of buzz from it. You lot are all so theoretical. Always very ideological. Always very serious. I don't trust people like you. A Doctor of Philosophy! Your heart's not in it.

He busies himself and whistles.

Chorus
  We are prepared
  The hoses carefully rolled
  According to colour,
  According to rule.
  Every hose reel
  Shining and carefully oiled.
  Everyone knows what has to be done.

Leader

It's only a pity the wind's coming up,
The wind from the south.

Chorus

Everyone knows what has to be done
The brass pumps, gleaming,
Have all been carefully checked
To make sure the pressure is high.

Leader

And remember to check on the hydrants.

Chorus

Everyone knows what has to be done.

Leader

We are prepared.

Enter the **Doctor** *and* **Babette**, *carrying a goose.*

Babette   Yes, Doctor, yes, I know it's urgent, I'll tell my husband it's urgent.

She leaves the **Doctor** *and comes downstage, holding up the goose.*

Babette   One goose. As ordered by husband. Apparently I'm meant to cook it so we can be friends with those two up there.

We hear church bells.

I can't get rid of this stupid feeling that it could be the last time the bells of this town will ring out like that . . .

Biedermann (*off*)   Babette!

Babette   I'm not sure my husband's always right. Honestly, I'm not. I mean, his line is, they may be thugs, but if he makes enemies of them, that's the end of his hair rejuvenator.

Biedermann (*off*)   Babette!

Babette   It's always the same. I know my Gottlieb. He's always too kind. Too kind for his own good.

She leaves, still carrying the goose.

Chorus
> Look at the one with the glasses,
> Probably son of a well-to-do family,
> Never known envy
> Probably very well read
> And horribly pale.
> Not one to hope that good might come
> From being good-natured,
> No, this one's ready
> To do just about anything,
> The end justifying the means
> (So he hopes).
> Respectable sometimes,
> Cleaning his glasses
> He's very far-sighted.
> In drums full of petrol
> He does not see petrol
> Instead he sees an idea.
> Till the idea's on fire.

Doctor   Good evening . . .

Leader
> Stand by the hoses!
> Stand by the pumps!
> Stand by the ladders!

The **Firemen** *run to their positions.*

Leader
> Good evening.

Fireman One
> Ready!

Fireman Two
> Ready!

Fireman Three
> Ready!

Leader
> We are prepared.

Scene Five

Living room.

Mrs Knechtling *is still there. She is standing. We hear church bells, very loud.*

Anna *is setting the table.* **Biedermann** *brings two chairs.*

Biedermann – because, as you see, I don't have time to deal with the dead, I don't have the time. You heard what I said: talk to my lawyer.

Mrs Knechtling *leaves.*

Biedermann   Anna, I can't hear myself think. Shut that window!

Anna *shuts the window and the bells are quieter.*

Biedermann   I said a cosy little meal. Why those ridiculous candlesticks?

Anna   We always have them, Mr Biedermann.

Biedermann   A cosy little meal, I said. None of this pretension. Oh my God, finger bowls! And porcelain plates! And a salt grinder, for God's sake! Everything's all white and elegant! What kind of impression does that make?

He picks up the salt grinder and puts it in his trouser pocket.

Oh, and Anna, I'm wearing my oldest jacket. But just look at you . . . You can keep the big carving knife, we'll need that. But apart from that, get rid of the smart stuff. Our two guests need to feel comfortable. Where's the corkscrew?

Anna   Here.

Biedermann   Don't we have anything simpler?

Anna   In the kitchen. But it's rusty.

Biedermann   Get it.

He takes a silver ice bucket off the table.

What's this doing here?

Anna   For the wine.

Biedermann   It's silver!

He stares at the ice bucket, then at **Anna**.

Do we always have this?

Anna   Yes. We need it, Mr Biedermann.

Biedermann   Need it? In what sense, need? What we need is a little human kindness, a sense of community. Get rid of it. And – what the hell are those?

Anna   Napkins.

Biedermann   Linen napkins!

Anna   They're the only ones we have.

He collects up the napkins and puts them in the ice bucket.

Biedermann   There are entire tribes who live without napkins, you know. People like us are –

Babette *enters with a large wreath.* **Biedermann** *fails to see her at first, stands in front of the table.*

Biedermann   I'm just wondering if we really need a tablecloth.

Babette   Gottlieb?

Biedermann   Let's make it classless.

He sees **Babette**.

Biedermann   What's the wreath for?

Babette   It's the one we ordered, Gottlieb. And what do you think? They've sent it here by mistake. I wrote out the address of the Knechtlings for them myself, clear as day. And the ribbon's all wrong.

Biedermann   The ribbon? Why?

Babette   And apparently they've sent the bill to Mrs Knechtling.

She shows him the ribbon.

Biedermann (*reading*)   'Gottlieb Biedermann. RIP'?! I'm sorry, this is unacceptable. It's bloody outrageous. They'll just have to change it.

He goes back to the table.

Don't get me all upset, now, Babette, I have other things to do, for God's sake. I can't be everywhere.

Babette *leaves with the wreath.*

Biedermann   Right, get rid of the tablecloth. Come on, Anna, give me a hand! And like I said, you don't dish out the food. Is that clear? You just come in without knocking, you just come in and you simply put the pan down on the table.

Anna   The pan? On the table?

Biedermann (*taking the tablecloth away*)   A completely different atmosphere, see? A wooden table, nothing more. Like at the last supper.

He gives her the tablecloth.

Anna   You mean you want me to bring the goose to the table in the roasting pan?

She folds up the tablecloth.

What wine do you want?

Biedermann   I'll get it myself.

Anna   Mr Biedermann!

Biedermann   What is it now?

Anna   I don't have a jumper. At least not the kind you want me to wear so that I look like one of the family.

Biedermann   Borrow one from my wife.

Anna   The yellow or the red?

Biedermann   Just keep it informal! I don't want to see any caps or aprons, is that understood? And like I said, get rid of the candlesticks. And generally, just make sure the place doesn't look so perfect. I'll be down in the cellar.

He leaves.

Anna   'Just make sure the place doesn't look so perfect.' All right then.

Anna *flings the tablecloth into a corner, goes over and tramples it as* **Schmitz** *and* **Eisenring** *enter, each carrying a rose.*

Schmitz *and* **Eisenring**   Good evening.

Anna *leaves without looking at them.*

Eisenring   And why are there no firelighters?

Schmitz   They've all been seized by the police. A pre-emptive measure. Anyone selling or possessing firelighters without a licence will be arrested. A pre-emptive national security measure.

He combs his hair.

Eisenring   Have you got a light?

Schmitz   No.

Eisenring   Me neither.

Schmitz (*blowing his comb clean*)   We'll have to ask him.

Eisenring   What, Biedermann?

Schmitz   Yes. Don't forget.

He puts his comb away. He sniffs

Mmm, smells good.

Biedermann *enters downstage, bottles in his arms.*

Biedermann (*to audience*)   You can think what you like about me, all right? But tell me this –

Schmitz *and* **Eisenring** *shout and laugh.*

Biedermann   Sorry about those two. But if that's all they get up to, I'll be happy. If someone had told me a week ago that I'd be getting the best bottles out of my cellar . . . for them! . . . Now, come on, tell me the truth: exactly how long have you known that those two are arsonists? It's not like you think. It doesn't dawn on you just like that. It starts slowly, and then suddenly: suspicion. Well, I had my suspicions right from the start, you always have your suspicions, don't you? But be honest, in my place, what would you have done? Come on, for God's sake, what would you have done?! And when?

He listens.

Silence.

I've got to go.

He hurries off.

Scene Six

Living room.

The goose supper is in full swing. **Biedermann**, *holding a bottle, is doubled up with laughter at the joke that has just been told.* **Schmitz** *and* **Eisenring** *join in the laughter, but* **Babette** *does not.*

Biedermann   Kindling? Did you hear that one? Kindling. With kindling you don't really need firelighters!

Babette   Why's that funny?

Biedermann   Do you know what kindling is?

Babette   Yes. You light fires with it.

Biedermann   You have no sense of humour, Babette.

He puts the bottle on the table.

What can you do with someone who simply has no sense of humour?

Babette   Then explain the joke.

Biedermann   All right. So, this morning, Billy says he's sent Joe to steal some firelighters. Firelighters, right? And so I ask Joe, what's this with firelighters? And he says, he couldn't find any firelighters, only bags of kindling. You understand? And Billy says, with kindling, you don't really need firelighters!

Babette   I understood that.

Biedermann   Did you?

Babette   Yes. Only it isn't funny.

Biedermann (*giving up on her*)   Come on, let's have a drink!

He opens the bottle.

Babette (*to* **Schmitz**)   Is it true then? Have you got bags of kindling up in our attic?

Biedermann   You'll laugh, Babette. This morning we even measured out the fuse wire together, me and Billy.

Babette   The fuse wire?

Biedermann   Detonating fuse wire.

He fills the glasses.

Babette   Seriously though, please, everyone. What's going on?

Biedermann (*laughs*)   'Seriously though,' she says! 'Seriously though.' Did you hear that, 'seriously though'? They're winding you up, Babette. They have a slightly offbeat sense of humour. Some jokes travel, some don't, that's what I always say. I expect you'll be asking me for a light next!

Schmitz *and* **Eisenring** *exchange glances.*

Biedermann   You see, our two guests still think I'm an uptight little coward. With no sense of humour. The sort of person who'll believe anything.

He raises his glass.

Cheers!

Eisenring   Cheers!

Schmitz   Cheers!

They clink glasses.

Biedermann   To our friendship.

They stand to drink and sit down again.

Please. Help yourself. Don't wait to be served. It's not that kind of house.

Schmitz   I can't eat any more.

Eisenring   Don't hold back. You're not in the orphanage now, Joe. Don't hold back.

He helps himself to goose.

Your goose is terrific, Babette,

Babette   I'm delighted.

Eisenring (*relishing the red wine*)   Goose with a decent burgundy . . . mmm. All we really need now is a tablecloth.

Babette   Gottlieb, did you hear that?

Eisenring   It's not essential. You know, a nice white linen tablecloth, with candlesticks.

Biedermann   Anna!

Eisenring   Perhaps damask linen? With a floral pattern? White flowers, of course. Something delicate, like those frost patterns you see on windowpanes. But it's not essential, Gottlieb, it's not essential. In prison we didn't have tablecloths either.

Biedermann   Anna!

Babette   In prison?!

Biedermann   Where on earth is she?

Babette   Have you been in prison?

Anna *enters, in a bright red jumper.*

Biedermann   Anna, bring a tablecloth. Right away.

Anna   Very good.

Eisenring   You don't happen to have finger bowls, do you?

Anna   Of course.

Eisenring   And perhaps a few serviettes? Or does one say napkins?

Anna   Of course.

Eisenring   You may find it childish, Babette, but ordinary people are like that, I'm afraid. Take Joe, father a miner, never seen a salt grinder in his life – well, of course it's the dream of his poor, wasted life to sit at a table with nice cutlery and crystal glasses.

Babette   Oh, we can provide that.

Eisenring   But it's not essential.

Anna   Fine.

Anna *brings everything to the table.*

Eisenring   I hope you're not taking this the wrong way, Babette. You know, when you're fresh out of prison, deprived of cultivated society for months on end –

He takes the tablecloth and shows it to **Schmitz**.

Eisenring   Do you know what this is? (*To* **Babette**.) Never seen one in his life. (*Back to* **Schmitz**.) This is linen. Damask linen.

Schmitz   So? What am I meant to do with it?

Eisenring *ties the tablecloth around* **Schmitz**'s *neck.*

Eisenring   Like this.

Biedermann *tries to find it funny, laughs.*

Babette   And where's our nice salt grinder, Anna?

Anna   Mr Biedermann said –

Biedermann   Get it!

Anna   You said, get rid of it.

Biedermann No, get it! That's what I'm saying! Where in God's name is it?!

Anna In your left-hand trouser pocket.

Biedermann *puts his hand into his pocket and finds it.*

Eisenring Calm down, now.

Anna Well, it's not my fault!

Eisenring Calm down.

Anna *bursts into tears, turns and leaves.*

Eisenring It's the weather. You know, wind from the south.

Pause.

Biedermann Come on, friends, drink up!

They drink in silence.

Eisenring I used to have goose every day, of course. When I was a waiter. You know, dashing down those long corridors, plateful of goose right there in the palm of my hand . . . well . . . you know. But then, of course, afterwards, where do you wipe your fingers? That's the question. Answer: in your hair. And to think other people have crystal finger bowls for that! That's what I can't get out of my mind. The crystal finger bowls.

He dips his fingers into the finger bowl.

Do you know what it is to be traumatised?

Biedermann No.

Eisenring They explained it all to me in prison.

He dries his fingers.

Babette How did you end up in prison?

Biedermann Babette!

Eisenring How did I end up in prison?

Biedermann You don't ask people things like that.

Eisenring   I often ask myself the same question. Like I said, I was a waiter. A little head waiter. And then, out of the blue, they mistook this little head waiter for a big-time arsonist.

Biedermann   Hmm.

Eisenring   Arrested me in my own home.

Biedermann   Hmm.

Eisenring   I was so taken aback, I went along with it.

Biedermann   Hmm.

Eisenring   I was lucky, Babette. They sent seven extremely charming policemen. When I explained that I had to get to the restaurant and had no time to talk to them, they said the restaurant had been burnt down.

Biedermann   Burnt down?

Eisenring   Yes. During the night, apparently.

Babette   Burnt down?

Eisenring   Fine, I said. In that case I have got time. The restaurant was just a pile of smouldering timbers. I saw it as we drove past, you know, from the little barred window in the police van.

He drinks his wine like a connoisseur.

Biedermann   And then?

Eisenring (*examining the wine label*)   Cave de l'Echanson. We used to have this in the restaurant, you know. Good year, too. And anyway, there I am sitting in the police station, fiddling with my handcuffs, and who do they bring in but him!

Schmitz *beams.*

Eisenring   Cheers, Joe!

Schmitz   Cheers, Billy!

They drink.

Biedermann   And then?

Schmitz   'Are you the arsonist?' they ask him, and offer him a cigarette. And he says, 'Excuse me, officer, even though you think I'm an arsonist I'm afraid I don't have a light.'

They laugh uproariously and slap their thighs.

Biedermann   Hmm.

Anna *enters. She is once again wearing a maid's outfit. She hands* **Biedermann** *a business card, which he examines.*

Anna   He says it's urgent.

Biedermann   But I've got guests –

Schmitz *and* **Eisenring** *clink glasses again.*

Schmitz   Cheers, Billy!

Eisenring   Cheers, Joe!

They drink. **Biedermann** *examines the business card again.*

Babette   Who is it, then, Gottlieb?

Biedermann   It's that Doctor of Philosophy.

Anna *busies herself at the sideboard.*

Eisenring   And what about those other things over there?

Anna   The candlesticks?

Eisenring   Why are you hiding them away?

Biedermann   Bring them over!

Anna   But, Mr Biedermann, you told me to –

Biedermann   I said, bring them over!

Anna *puts the candlesticks on the table.*

Eisenring   Joe, can you imagine? They have these beautiful candlesticks and they hide them away! Got any matches?

He digs in his trouser pocket.

Schmitz   Me? No.

He also digs in his trouser pocket.

Eisenring   Sad to say, we don't have any matches.

Biedermann   Ah, but I do.

Eisenring   Let's have them, then!

Biedermann   No, no, no, allow me. Allow me.

He lights the candles.

Babette   What's he want, this doctor of philosophy?

Anna   I don't know what he's on about, madam. He's waiting on the stairs. Says he can no longer be silent.

Babette   He wants to speak to my husband in private?

Anna   Yes. He says he wishes to expose a scandal.

Babette   What kind of scandal?

Anna   I don't understand a word he says, Mrs Biedermann. He could say it a hundred times and I still wouldn't understand it. Something about wanting to disassociate himself from . . .

Lots of candles have been lit.

Eisenring   You can't beat candlelight for atmosphere, can you? Don't you agree, Babette?

Babette   Yes. Yes, it's true.

Eisenring   I'm all for atmosphere.

Biedermann   Absolutely.

Now all the candles have been lit.

Eisenring   Schmitz! Table manners!

Babette *takes* **Eisenring** *aside.*

Babette   Leave him alone.

Eisenring   He has absolutely no manners, Babette. Eats like a pig. I am so sorry. I'm simply appalled. But then, how could he have table manners? From coalminer's cottage to children's home to . . . well . . .

Babette   I know, I know.

Eisenring   From children's home to the circus.

Babette   I know.

Eisenring   From the circus to the theatre.

Babette   I know. (*Beat.*) The theatre?!

Eisenring   Fate, Babette, fate.

Babette *turns to* **Schmitz**.

Babette   Were you in the theatre?

Schmitz *gnaws at a goose bone and nods.*

Babette   Where?

Schmitz   Backstage.

Eisenring   But very talented. Have you seen him do his ghost?

Schmitz   No, no, not now.

Eisenring   Why not?

Schmitz   I was only in the theatre for a week when it burnt down.

Babette   Burnt down?!

Eisenring   Come on, don't be shy.

Biedermann   Burnt down?

Eisenring   Don't be shy.

He takes off the cloth that has been worn by **Schmitz** *as a napkin, and throws it over* **Schmitz**'s *head.*

Eisenring   Come on!

Schmitz, *with white cloth over his head, stands up.*

Eisenring   See what I mean? Terrific ghost.

Anna   It's a bit scary.

Eisenring   Aw, poor baby!

Eisenring *tries to put his arm round* **Anna**, *who covers her face with her hands.*

Schmitz   Settle down, everybody!

Eisenring   Theatre language, Babette. He learned that after only a week of rehearsals. Amazing, eh? Of course, that was before the fire.

Babette   Will you stop talking about fires!

Schmitz   Settle down, everybody!

Eisenring   Ready?

The others remain seated as **Eisenring** *pulls* **Anna** *towards him.*

Schmitz   Everyman! Everyman!

Babette   Gottlieb?

Biedermann   Shush.

Babette   Didn't we see this at Stratford?

Biedermann (*snaps*)   Salzburg!

Babette   Salzburg.

Schmitz   Biedermann! Biedermann!

Eisenring   Terrific performance, eh?

Schmitz   Biedermann! Biedermann!

Eisenring   You have to ask, 'Who are you?'

Biedermann   Me?

Eisenring   Otherwise he can't do his big speech.

Biedermann   Oh, all right. Who am I?

Babette   No, you've got to ask who *he* is!

Biedermann   Oh, I see.

Schmitz   Dost thou not hear me?

Eisenring   No, Joe, stop. Take it from the top. That's another theatrical expression.

They take up different positions.

Schmitz   Everyman! Biedermann!

Babette   Let me guess. Are you meant to be Death?

Biedermann   Don't be stupid.

Babette   Well, what else can he be?

Biedermann   You're meant to ask, who are you? He could be Hamlet's father. Or Banquo. Or that stone statue, you know, what's-his-name, in *Don Giovanni*?

Schmitz   Who calls me?

Eisenring   Keep going.

Schmitz   Biedermann! Biedermann!

Babette   Go on, ask him, he's talking to you.

Schmitz   Dost thou not hear me?

Biedermann   All right, then, who are you?

Schmitz   I am the ghost of . . . Knechtling!

Babette *jumps up. She screams.*

Eisenring   Stop!

He tears the cloth off **Schmitz***'s head.*

Eisenring   You moron! Knechtling! You can't play the ghost of Knechtling! It's not on! Knechtling was buried today.

Schmitz   Exactly.

Babette *covers her face with her hands.*

Eisenring   Mrs Biedermann, don't worry, it's not him.

He shakes his head at **Schmitz***.*

Eisenring   How could you be so tasteless?

Schmitz   I couldn't think of who else to be.

Eisenring   Knechtling! What a choice. An old colleague of Mr Biedermann's, a faithful employee, just think about it, laid to rest this very day. Corpse still in perfect condition. White as a tablecloth. Pale and gleaming like damask, cold, and stiff. And you decide to put him on the stage!

*He takes **Babette** by the shoulders.*

Eisenring   Word of honour, Mrs Biedermann, that was not Knechtling.

Schmitz (*wiping sweat from his face*)   I'm sorry.

Biedermann   Let's all sit down.

Anna   Is that it?

They sit down. An awkward pause.

Biedermann   How about a little cigar?

He offers a box of cigars.

Eisenring   How stupid can you be? Look, go on, look at poor Mr Biedermann. He's trembling all over. (*Taking cigar.*) Thank you, Mr Biedermann, most kind. I suppose you think it's funny? When you know very well that Knechtling put his head in an oven, forgetting everything that Gottlieb had done for him? Fourteen years Mr Biedermann gave that man work, fourteen years, and what thanks does he get for it?

Biedermann   Let's not talk about it any more.

Eisenring   That's your thank you.

They prepare their cigars.

Schmitz   Shall I sing us a song?

Eisenring   What song?

Schmitz   Um, let me see . . .

He sings.

London's burning, London's burning.

Eisenring   That's enough.

Schmitz
Fetch the engines, fetch the engines.
Fire, fire! Fire, fire!

Eisenring   He's drunk.

Schmitz (*fumbling with his flies*)
Pour on wee-wee, pour on wee-wee.

Eisenring   Don't listen, Mrs Biedermann.

Schmitz
Pour on wee-wee, pour on wee-wee.

He starts again.

London's burning, London's burning . . .

Biedermann   'Pour on wee-wee . . . ' That's good.

The round continues, with **Biedermann** *and* **Schmitz** *joining in.*

The Men
London's burning, London's burning,
Fetch the engines, fetch the engines,
Fire, fire! Fire, fire!
Pour on water, pour on water.

Amid lots of noise and laughter, they continue with the round. Every now and then they pause, but it is always **Biedermann** *who sets it off again, leading the fun, until everyone is exhausted.*

Biedermann   Well then . . . cheers!

They raise their glasses. Off: distant sirens.

Biedermann   What was that?

Eisenring   Sirens.

Biedermann   No, joking apart.

Babette   It's the arsonists, that's what it is, the arsonists!

Biedermann   Don't shout.

Babette *tears the window open. We hear sirens get nearer. The shrieking noise pierces to the quick as they go howling past.*

Biedermann   At least they're not for us.

Babette   Where are they heading?

Eisenring   Where the south wind comes from.

Biedermann   At least they're not for us.

Eisenring   It's our normal procedure. We set off a false alarm in some poor district on the outskirts of town, and later, when everything's really hotting up, they find their way back has been blocked.

Biedermann   But joking apart . . .

Schmitz   But that's how we do it. Joking apart.

Biedermann   Let's just stop the nonsense. Please! There's a limit. Look at my wife. She's as white as a sheet.

Schmitz   As a tablecloth.

Babette (*to* **Biedermann**)   You don't look so good yourself.

Biedermann   After all, a siren is a siren, it's not something I find funny. There are limits. And there's a fire out there somewhere. There's a fire. Otherwise the fire brigade wouldn't be out.

Eisenring *looks at his watch.*

Eisenring   We have to go.

Biedermann   What, already?

Eisenring   I'm afraid so.

Schmitz
Fetch the engine, fetch the engine,
Fire, fire! Fire, fire!

We can hear the sirens again.

Biedermann   Let's have coffee, Babette.

Babette *leaves.*

Biedermann   And you, Anna? Don't just stand there with your mouth open!

Anna *leaves.*

Biedermann   Just between us, enough is enough. My wife has a heart condition. I'd like you to stop joking about people setting fire to things.

Schmitz   Oh, but we're not joking.

Eisenring   We're arsonists.

Biedermann   Now listen – and I'm very serious about this –

Schmitz   We're very serious.

Eisenring   Very serious.

Schmitz   Why don't you believe us?

Eisenring   Your house is in a perfect position, Mr Biedermann. Don't you realise that? You'll be one of five fires. All in a circle round the petrol station. You see, we can't attack the petrol stations directly, because they're guarded now. But with fires all around, and the south wind blowing, well . . .

Biedermann   I don't believe it.

Schmitz   Gottlieb. If you really think we're arsonists, why not say so?

Biedermann *nods like a whipped dog*

Biedermann   It's not that I think you're arsonists, that's not true. You do me an injustice. I don't think you're . . . arsonists.

Eisenring   You swear?

Biedermann   I swear, I swear you're not arsonists!

Schmitz   Who do you think we are, then?

Biedermann   You're . . . you're my friends.

They clap him on the shoulder and leave him standing there.

Where are you going now?

Eisenring   It's time.

Biedermann   I swear. As God is my witness.

Eisenring   God?

Biedermann   Yes!

He slowly raises his hand as if taking an oath.

Schmitz   Billy doesn't believe in God. And neither do you. So you can swear as long as you like.

They continue to the door.

Biedermann   What can I do to make you believe me?

He blocks their exit.

Eisenring   Give us your matches.

Biedermann   What? I'm meant to – ?

Eisenring   We're right out of matches.

Biedermann   I'm meant to – ?

Eisenring   If you don't think we're arsonists . . .

Biedermann   Matches?

Schmitz   As a sign of trust.

Eisenring   A lighter will do.

Biedermann *puts his hand into his trouser pocket.*

Eisenring   He's not sure. Can you see? He's not sure.

Biedermann   Quiet. Not in front of my wife . . .

Babette (*entering*)   Coffee will be ready in a moment.

Pause.

You're leaving?

Biedermann   Well, my friends, it's a great pity, but . . . well, the main thing is, you have realised that we – I don't want to make any big speeches, but, well, why don't we use first names?

Babette   Hmm.

Biedermann   And drink a toast to friendship.

He picks up a bottle and the corkscrew.

Eisenring   Tell your husband he shouldn't open another bottle on our account. It's really not worth it now.

Biedermann (*uncorking the bottle*)   Nothing's too much trouble for you, my friends, nothing's too much trouble. Anything you'd like, anything at all . . . just say.

He hastily fills the glasses and hands them round.

A toast.

They clink glasses.

To friendship.

*He kisses **Schmitz** on the cheek.*

Biedermann   Joe.

Schmitz   Gottlieb.

Biedermann *kisses* **Eisenring** *on the cheek.*

Biedermann   Billy.

Eisenring   Gottlieb.

They stand and drink.

Eisenring   Time to go, I'm afraid.

Schmitz   Must be off.

Eisenring   Babette . . .

We hear sirens.

Babette   It was a delightful evening.

We hear church bells ringing in alarm.

Eisenring   Oh, one more thing, Gottlieb.

Biedermann   What?

Eisenring   I think you know.

Biedermann   If there's anything you'd like me to do . . .

Eisenring   The matches.

Anna *has come in with the coffee.*

Babette   Anna, what's wrong?

Anna   Coffee.

Babette   You're all upset.

Anna   If you look out the back . . . The sky . . . from the kitchen window, you can see it . . . the whole sky is lit up.

The sky is already red as **Schmitz** *and* **Eisenring** *bow and leave.*

Biedermann *stands pale and stiff.*

Biedermann   Well, it's not our house, at least it's not our house.

The **Doctor of Philosophy** *enters.*

Biedermann   What do you want?

Doctor   I can no longer be silent.

Takes document from his jacket pocket and reads:

'I the undersigned, being deeply distressed by recent events, events which in my view can only be regarded as criminal, wish to make the following statement . . . '

We hear howling of many sirens, as the **Doctor** *reads out a detailed text, of which not a single word can be heard. It is drowned out by the barking of dogs, alarm bells, shouts and screams, far-off sirens and, closer, the crackling of flames. Then the* **Doctor** *crosses to* **Biedermann** *and gives him the document.*

Doctor   I completely disassociate myself from it all.

Biedermann   And?

Doctor   I have said what I have to say.

He takes his glasses off and folds them away.

You see, Mr Biedermann, I was a do-gooder. Earnest and honest. I knew exactly what they were doing up in your attic, every detail of it. But there was one thing I didn't know – they do it because they like doing it.

Biedermann Doctor –

The **Doctor** *withdraws.*

Biedermann Listen, you – Doctor – What am I meant to do with this?

The **Doctor** *goes downstage and into the auditorium, where he takes a seat in the stalls.*

Babette Gottlieb . . .

Biedermann He's gone.

Babette What did you give them? I saw you. Was it matches? Was it?

Biedermann Well . . . why not?

Babette You gave them matches?

Biedermann Yes. If they have no matches of their own, they can't possibly be arsonists, can they? Babette . . . My darling Babette . . .

The grandfather clock strikes. Silence. The light gets redder. As it gets dark onstage we hear alarm bells, dogs barking, sirens, the noise of collapsing buildings, car horns, crackling of flames, shouts, until the **Chorus** *enters.*

Chorus
There is much that is senseless
And nothing more senseless
Than the story just told.
A story once started
That killed many people,
But didn't kill everyone
And failed to change anything.

First explosion.

Leader

First storage tank.

Second explosion.

Leader

Second storage tank.

Chorus

If you spend long enough
Looking into the future
What you foresee
Will finally happen:
Stupidity dressed up as fate,
Always stupidity
Blazing and burning
Until it can not be put out.

Third explosion.

Leader

Another storage tank.

There follows a series of horrific explosions.

Chorus

Woe unto us.

House lights up. Curtain.